BURN AFTER READING

somebody get me a match

BURN AFTER READING

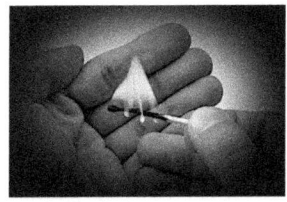

VOLUME 1 ///
MINIATURE MANIFESTOS FOR A POST/MEDIEVAL
STUDIES

Eileen A. Joy and Myra Seaman, editors

VOLUME 2 ///
THE FUTURE WE WANT: A COLLABORATION

Jeffrey Jerome Cohen, editor

with the assistance of Paul J. Megna

a joint production of

punctum books ∗ brooklyn, ny

Oliphaunt Books | Washington, DC

Burn After Reading

Vol. 1. Miniature Manifestos for a Post/medieval Studies

Vol. 2. The Future We Want: A Collaboration

©Jeffrey Jerome Cohen, Eileen A. Joy, and Myra Seaman, 2014.

http://creativecommons.org/licenses/by-nc-nd/3.0

This work is Open Access, which means that you are free to copy, distribute, display, and perform the work as long as you clearly attribute the work to the authors, that you do not use this work for commercial gain in any form whatsoever, and that you in no way alter, transform, or build upon the work outside of its normal use in academic scholarship without express permission of the author and the publisher of this volume.

First published jointly in 2014 by:

punctum books
Brooklyn, New York
punctumbooks.com

Oliphaunt Books
Washington, DC
www.oliphauntbooks.com

ISBN-13: 978-0692204412
ISBN-10: 0692204415

Facing-page drawing by Heather Masciandaro.

Agents of chaos cast burning glances at anything or anyone capable of bearing witness to their condition, their fever of *lux et voluptas*.

Hakim Bey, *Temporary Autonomous Zone*

TABLE OF CONTENTS

VOL. 1 ///
MINIATURE MANIFESTOS FOR A POST/MEDIEVAL STUDIES

Prefatory Note: Manifest This!
Eileen A. Joy

1/
Intentionally Good, Really Bad
Heather Bamford

5/
21st-Century Medieval Studies:
Seeing a Forest as Well as Trees
Frank Battaglia

9/
Net Worth
Bettina Bildhauer

13/
Our Feminism/Our Activism
Martha Easton + Maggie Williams

19/
Be Critical!
Ruth Evans

25/
This Is Your Brain on Medieval Studies
Joshua R. Eyler

29/
Sticking Together
Lara Farina

37/
Waging Guerrilla Warfare Against the 19th Century
Matthew Gabriele

41/
Medieval Studies in the Subjunctive Mood
Gaelan Gilbert

47/
Radical Ridicule
Noah D. Guynn

53/
Burn(ed) Before Writing: The Late Stages of a
Late Medieval PhD and Current Academic Realities
David Hadbawnik

59/
History and Commitment
Guy Halsall

63/
On Never Letting Go
Cary Howie

73/
The Gothic Fly
Shayne Aaron Legassie

79/
Fuck Postcolonialism
Erin Maglaque

85/
We Are the Material Collective
Material Collective

89/
Medievalism/Surrealism
Thomas Mical

97/
De catervis ceteris
Chris Piuma

101/
2nd Program of the Ornamentalists
Daniel C. Remein

105/
A Medieval: Manifesto
Christopher Roman

109/
Homo Narrans
Eva von Contzen

113/
Historicism and its Discontents
Erik Wade

119/
'Tis Magick, Magick That Will Have Ravished Me
Lisa Weston

VOL. 2 ///
THE FUTURE WE WANT: A COLLABORATION

Prefatory Note: The Future We Want
Jeffrey Jerome Cohen

127/
Field Change/Discipline Change
Anne Harris + Karen Overbey

145/
Paradigm Change/Institute Change
L.O. Aranye Fradenburg + Eileen A. Joy

157/
Time Change/Mode Change
Allan Mitchell + Will Stockton

165/
World Change/Sea Change
Lowell Duckert + Steve Mentz

177/
Voice Change/Language Change
Jonathan Hsy + Chris Piuma

189/
Mood Change/Collective Change
Julian Yates + Julie Orlemanski

BURN AFTER READING

Volume 1
Miniature Manfestos for a
Post/medieval Studies

Prefatory Note

MANIFEST THIS!

Eileen A. Joy

> . . . better to take the risk and engage in fidelity to a Truth-event, even if it ends in catastrophe, than to vegetate in the eventless utilitarian-hedonist survival of what Nietzsche called the 'last men.'
>
> Slavoj Žižek, *Living in the End Times*

The manifestos (and also anti-manifestos) collected here are culled from sessions organized by the BABEL Working Group and *postmedieval: a journal of medieval cultural studies* at the 2012 International Congress on Medieval Studies (Kalamazoo, MI), for which sessions we asked presenters to contemplate and "manifest" alternative futures for a post/medieval studies, as well as what it means to "let go" of something ("fuck this") and/or "never let go" ("fuck me"). The presentations were, alternately and simultaneously, bracing, funny, sad, provocative, hopeful, pessimistic, sexy, lyrical, polemical, playful, political, amorous, subjunctive, sticky, frustrated, materialist, dejected, angry, surrealist, anti-nostalgic, activist, critical, tender, weird, and even alchemical.

It is to manifesting ourselves (making ourselves more present to each other, which is to also say, more responsible to each other) in some sort of collective endeavor that works on behalf of the future without laying any belligerent claims upon it, that we might craft new spaces for our so-called "premodern" studies, which is also, hopefully, a profession-at-large that would want to wander, that can never just be *some*where, dwelling in the partitive—of a particular place—but rather, seeks to be everywhere, always on the move, pandemic, uncontainable, and yes, precarious, always at risk. While also always being present between us (manifest).

Manifesting ourselves (and our studies) requires persons willing to actually dream something different into being—something that might foster the production of knowledge while also somehow escaping the techno-managerial-bureaucratic capture of everything. And we have to stop saying (and believing) it's really hard to work with others: it is, but you just have to fucking do it, regardless. It would be a lot easier to keep one's head down and just concentrate on one's own, individual "work," but you'll get sucked up in the neoliberal vacuum anyway, and you'll be amazed at the pleasures and enjoyment (and even love) that comes with collective endeavours, despite their agonies and headaches. And this way, when the ship goes down, we've got company, and we can put a band together for some last-night music.

Whether desiring a particular future or simply trying to determine, *how shall we live now?* (increasingly my own preferred orientation, but really, the two are steps in the same fruitful direction), one needs collaborators. Which is to say, I and the other rogues of the BABEL Working Group desire a future in the Now with others, which can be an *agon*, to be a sure, but a necessary, and even enjoyable one (if, by "enjoyment," we mean to exult in our own difficulties with others). It has to be deliberative, and (again) difficultly so, but we'll choose thriving (and yes, change, and struggling) in the present, over surviving into the future. It shouldn't be about, "can we keep all the stuff we have now ... forever?" so much as it might be about, how can we not just live through change, but be agents of our own changes?

Manifestos can be hackneyed, and even dangerous, especially when they assume a ground-clearing maneuver (i.e., whatever exists now must be destroyed to make way for the new), but I think we increasingly need them, because they help us to outline our commitments and desires in a (writerly) action that *presences* those commitments and desires. That is Step 1 (Step 2 would be doing something about it), but it is an important step. In the manifesto—albeit, in the manifesto (and even in the anti-manifesto) that does not desire the violence of erasing the past or the Other—we express in an always-fleeting yet still phenomenologically palpable present a radical form of desire that seeks an alteration of the status quo, and while the manifesto often looks, in retrospect, silly and hyperbolic and always unaware of the demise of its (vain? arrogant? unrealistic? insane?) hopes, there is something *sincere* about it. It presents a radical opening to (or window upon) the risk of a terrible (and possibly embarrassing) honesty. We could do worse than to be honest with each other. We could do worse than to actually want things that we haven't been told in advance to want. This is also a matter of contributing to the political imaginary that some believe is withering away.

This volume is therefore not really a book; it is, rather, a blueprint, or perhaps, for the future reader, a record of foolish, yet brave, articulations. More importantly, however, this is a gathering, a rave, in the present, a commitment to simply being together, for better or worse, in the always precarious tense of the present, while laboring to craft a "something else." Perhaps that "something else" is already here, already manifest. In which case, please inhabit your present tenses. They look good on you.

Eileen A. Joy
University of California, Santa Barbara

# 01/

INTENTIONALLY GOOD, REALLY BAD

Heather Bamford

The epigraph for this miniature manifesto is a line that a friend and I remembered as hers. It turned out that that attribution was only part true, since it is also something that Derrida said of Hélène Cixous when they committed her work to the National Library of France:

The door is barred but please come in.[1]

I hope medieval studies will conceptualize intention when writing about medieval manuscript culture. I don't

---

[1] Jacques Derrida, *Geneses, Genealogies, Genres, and Genius: The Secrets of the Archive*, trans. Beverley Bie Brahic (New York: Columbia University Press, 2006), 46.

mean the intentions of medieval authors, but intentions that could seem just as objectionable: those of the medieval people who used manuscripts. By manuscript culture, I refer not only to the reading and writing activities of multiple scribes and readers, but also to other uses of manuscripts, some of which today seem anti-intellectual for a variety of reasons, including purposeful destruction for use in binding, the extraction of leaves for sale or decorative use, and even the use of manuscript material as talismans.

My interest in the intentions of medieval users of manuscripts stems from research on manuscript fragments, pieces separated from their whole manuscripts. Because there were so many fragments, and because some were so sexy, but also so useless, I began to think that many of them came about intentionally, rather than as a result of accidents. I wondered about what sort of material, intellectual, and spiritual uses of manuscript material made the fragments fragments.

> I thought why, for instance, are the only extant folios of a certain Carolingian epic those that were sewn together to form a folder or bag?
>
> What lead to the purposeful erasure of the ten stanzas of a Latin epic about Rodrigo Díaz de Vivar?
>
> Why were folios torn from a Qur'an and hidden in the coffers of a medieval Islamic Palace?

It may seem crazy to invoke Derrida in anything to do with intention, and in a way it is. In a 1960s talk on Foucault's History of Madness, Descartes, and Freud, Derrida wrote that in order to read Descartes, it is for necessary to gain "a good understanding ... by taking into account what Descartes meant on the already so difficult surface of his text ... before and in order to destabilize it." In that same talk, Derrida also said: "Whatever one ends up doing with it, one must begin by listening to the canon."[2]

Derrida might not have meant these statements ever again, or even when he said them the first time, but they make me wonder: what do we do when there is no canon, no standard by which to decode manuscript evidence that is strange or uncanny, or not the product of reading and writing? In the case of no canon, as is generally the case for the reasons why fragments came to be fragments, I think it is possible to entertain final cause, to think about the reasons why they were made fragments. That person who fashioned the folder or purse from two folios of the Carolingian epic needed a carrying device more than reading material. The Latin epic I mentioned was likely rendered a palimpsest for reasons of censorship. The folios torn or excerpted from the Qur'an were probably placed in the coffers to protect the people in the building, rather than to protect the folios themselves. All that is manuscript culture.

The fragment is the ultimate barred, but beckoning door. It asks us to ask it why it is here, in that partial state, without offering up much evidence with which we might answer. Breasts came up at a recent conference. A colleague stated that she'd love to write about a big-breasted lady in the margins of a manuscript, but lacked the whys and hows to write the article. Perhaps a renewed look at intention, not only the intentions of medieval manuscript users that created and used fragments, but those working whole manuscripts too, will lift the big bad bar on manuscript studies.

---

[2] Derrida, *Geneses, Genealogies, Genres, and Genius*, 84.

02/

21ST-CENTURY MEDIEVAL STUDIES
SEEING A FOREST AS WELL AS TREES

Frank Battaglia

Our subject, medieval studies, was named for a "middle age." It came between Antiquity, specifically the Roman Empire, and the nation states that succeeded it, particularly in Europe.

An extensive regime was displaced as competing structures of power—operating from various centers but often more elaborate in their controls—struggled into existence.

We live in a time when the so-called global economic system, enacted by free-range and state-run capitalisms, is extending its reach over the entire planet, dislocating national networks. International trade agreements diminish the ability of even the U.S. or E.U., let alone less powerful entities, to enforce environmental or labor laws.

Nation states are giving way to a larger system, difficult to describe, as the interests of the World Economic Forum impel events more effectively than those of the U.N. General Assembly.[1] Meanwhile, from Ecuadorean tribes of the upper Amazon to the adivasi of forest India, virtually no area escapes exploitation, nor does any independent social entity avoid integration and/or obliteration.[2]

The emerging global system is similar to an earlier one in which a Mediterranean empire came to control fifty million square miles of Europe, Africa and Asia. But whereas late Antiquity, and the medieval period, saw the disintegration of an older world system, we are witnessing creation of a new one.

Investigation of the middle between two systems is what we should be able to do. Better than many disciplines, medieval studies can interrogate the difference and sameness of the past. Roman rhetorician Cicero stated as a principle that, "The work of all hired men who sell their labor . . . is servile and contemptible. The reason is that in their case wages actually constitute a payment for slavery."[3] Like other surviving voices of the ancient Mediterranean world, Cicero considered servile labor (of oth-

---

[1] Indigenous peoples have articulated the principle of "restorative justice." See, for example, World People's Conference on Climate Change and the Rights of Mother Earth, "People's Agreement," April 22, 2010, Cochabamba, Bolivia: http://pwccc.wordpress.com/support/, which expresses the value of balance and community. The concept has seen some application in national and international jurisprudence—for example, see United Nations Office on Drugs and Crime, *Handbook on Restorative Justice Programs* (New York: United Nations, 2006); available online: http://www.unodc.org/pdf/criminal_justice/06-56290_Ebook.pdf.

[2] Arundhati Roy has aptly situated the "conversation" needed at this moment: *Walking with the Comrades* (New York: Penguin, 2011), 212–213.

[3] "Illiberales ... et sordidi quaestus mercennariorum omnium, quorum operae ... ; est enim in illis ipsa merces auctoramentum servitutis": Cicero, *De officiis*, 1, 42, 150. English translation from Aldo Schiavone, *The End of the Past: Ancient Rome and the Modern West*, trans. Margery J. Schneider (Cambridge, MA: Harvard University Press, 2000), 40.

ers, of course) to be "the unavoidable condition of civilized life."[4] Slavery, clearly, led to *The End of the Past*, but what future may be articulated from pervasive minimum-wage labor or unemployment with no access to land?

Encompassing system collapse and the generation of its replacements, medieval studies can illuminate the transformations of our own day. Counter-discourses existed in the medieval world just as they do in the contemporary one.[5] "The meaning of the past is political and belongs to the present."[6]

The "middle age" we profess interest in saw a dominant narrative de- and re-constructed. Surely that gives us some basis to understand and speak for human interests as extraction of value reaches the deep ocean floor, guided by communication nodes hovering in the sky, as new relationships connect inner and outer spaces.

"Postcolonial studies and medieval studies have interrelated genealogies."[7] They have, as well, interrelated projects.

---

[4] M.M. Austin, and P. Vidal-Naquet, *Economic and Social History of Ancient Greece: An Introduction*, 2nd edn. (Berkeley: University of California Press, 1977), 18.

[5] For a counter-narrative with gender, religious, and political dimensions found in Old Irish and Breton versions, see Frank Battaglia, "A Common Background to *Lai de Graelent* and *Noínden Ulad*?"" *Emania* 11 (1993): 41–48.

[6] Michael Shanks and Christopher Tilley, *Social Theory and Archaeology* (Cambridge, UK: Polity, 1987), 212.

[7] Lisa Lampert-Weissig, referring to the debt of South Asian postcolonial studies to the methodology of George Duby and others: *Medieval Literature and Postcolonial Studies* (Edinburgh University Press, 2010), 20.

03/

NET WORTH

Bettina Bildhauer

One might argue that we hardly need another plea for more materiality in medieval studies: it's a buzz topic at medievalist conferences; the first issue of *postmedieval* was devoted to it; and prominent members of the BABEL Working Group have been thinking with Bruno Latour, Jane Bennett, Bill Brown, and Graham Harman for years. And yet, the idea that agency is always an interaction, a network in which any element—not just what we traditionally call human subjects, but also non-human objects—can be alive, active and cognizant still sounds mad to the medievalist mainstream and to most of the general public. The subject-object distinction is one of our most basic patterns of thought and not easily displaced by academic fashion. So I will sound hopelessly belated and totally obvious to some, and crazily airy-fairy and nonsensical to others, when I now point out five things that I, as a literary and cultural historian, have learned so far from studying materiality.

Materiality is not the opposite of theory.
The new interest in materiality is often cast as nostalgia for the concrete world, for an assumed reality beneath the discourse, after the abstractions of theory and the rise of virtual reality. But for most recent medievalist work in this area, the interest in materiality comes precisely out of an engagement with feminist, ecofeminist, phenomenological, posthuman, and other theories, often based on an interest in bodies, gender and identity, and an embrace of new technologies for research and inspiration. The new wave of studies of things is not positivistic, but deeply theoretically informed, and there is nothing wrong with that.

Don't replace the subject with the object.
There's no point in just reversing the dominance of the human subject by substituting it with a concept of things as acting; no point in saying not that the grail knight finds the grail, but that the grail finds the knight. Instead, both let themselves be found. If we look closely at a grail romance such as Wolfram von Eschenbach's *Parzival*, the knight conquers but also has to be nominated as grail king; the grail is conquered but also nominates a conqueror. Neither humans nor things are presented as autonomous rational agents in the Enlightenment sense; agency is distributed across a network of agents modeled on humans, things, animals, gods, places and circumstances. It follows that:

Style matters.
There is a difference between saying, "Parzival decided to ride to the grail castle," and saying, "He let the reins go and spurred the horse; it went to the Forest of Salvation." In the first case, the grammatical subject and the entity who acts is Parzival; in the second, it's both Parzival and the horse, with the horse being the one who goes where it wants and finds the way to the grail. Only the second

passage is actually found in the grail romance. The way in which grammatical subject and object, as well as the functional actor and aim, are predominantly represented characterizes a text as deeply as whether it is told in prose or verse, by a first-person or third-person narrator. Popular stylistic techniques that ascribe agency to a network rather than to a human character include reporting outside forces as determining the actions of one character, splitting a character into different parts with equal agency, describing the *result* of an action rather than any conscious intention to carry it out, and emphasizing the metanarrative interaction between author, text and story as determining the plot.

Not every thing is the same.
Things want to be looked for in romances, exchanged in fabliaux, penetrated in epics, and adored in saints' lives. It pays to pay attention to which actions exactly objects perform, and what they are valued for—transparency, hardness, price, or rarity—in a particular text, image, genre, author, or period. Things may speak, but they all say different things. Finally:

There is no object of study.
If passive objects no longer exist within our sources, we've got to stop thinking of the sources themselves as objects, too. Medieval texts, images, and artifacts do not hold still for us to analyze them with a detached academic gaze, but look back, talk back, and interact with us, whether we like it or not.

04/

OUR FEMINISM/OUR ACTIVISM

Maggie M. Williams + Martha Easton

This is the transcript of a short collaborative presentation from the International Congress on Medieval Studies in Kalamazoo in May 2012. It was performed by Maggie M. Williams and Martha Easton, two founding members of the Material Collective (www.thematerialcollective.org). For us, the performance was an energizing moment of publicly calling for real activism, real feminism, real change in the academy, and we hope that its publication in this amazing little volume will give others the strength to "come out" as well.

Martha and I are mothers. We are feminists. We are art historians. We are activists. We have each struggled to keep those identities carefully compartmentalized to achieve some abstract notion of success. Both of us were drawn to BABEL's "Fuck This: On Finally Letting Go" and "Fuck Me: On Never Letting Go" sessions out of a sense of frustration: dissatisfaction with the tactics of purportedly activist groups, disillusionment with the hypocrisies of academic life, and disappointment in our own and others' willingness to rock the boat. Today, we are finally letting go of preserving our secret identities. Together, we will unmask our true selves, telling our stories and sharing our hopes for real change. Rather than coping silently, we want to call for real progressive action among medievalists.

We will be presenting a short performance piece that collages our experiences into a single narrative. We invite you to participate by chanting with us. (We'll tell you when!)

Martha:
I became a feminist the first day of fourth grade, when my teacher wrote "Ms. Wolman" on the board, not "Mrs." or "Miss" like the other teachers. By the time I was in college I was a committed organizer and activist. I chaired a newly-formed committee on sexual harassment and physical violence, organized protests against the Solomon Amendment which tied draft registration to financial aid, and agitated for the nuclear freeze—a photo of me in full

regalia got picked up by the national wires and published in papers across the country.

Martha Easton at the nuclear arms freeze rally

Maggie:
Feminism was instinctive for me, but I was reserved and rather shy. I had never been an activist. About a month before I finished my dissertation, I went to my first union meeting. The moving testimony of my grad student colleagues flipped a switch in me, and before I knew it, I was leading hundreds of TAs and RAs out on strike.

Maggie: Hey hey, ho ho ...
Martha: ... the status quo has got to go!
Together: Hey hey, ho ho ... the status quo has got to go!
Audience: Hey hey, ho ho ... the status quo has got to go! (2x)

Martha:
In graduate school I joined WAC, the Women's Action Coalition, which formed in 1992 after the outrage sparked by the Clarence Thomas Supreme Court confirmation hearings. We participated in direct actions like protesting, together with the Guerilla Girls, the new SoHo branch of the Guggenheim Museum—not one woman was included in the opening exhibition. Around that time, my funding for graduate school got pulled because I married a lawyer,

while a fellow graduate student, a man, also married a lawyer and retained his.

Maggie:
Marching outside of those hallowed gates day after day, week after week, we built our own university. Physicists and philosophers, administrative assistants and art historians, together we confronted our love objects (Columbia, our research projects, our paychecks) and said, "FUCK THIS!" If we can't have fairness, we don't want academia. If we can't have transparency, we don't want scholarship. We needed to break the silence.

Maggie: Tell me what democracy looks like ...
Martha: ... this is what democracy looks like.
Together: TELL ME WHAT DEMOCRACY LOOKS LIKE ...
Audience: ... THIS IS WHAT DEMOCRACY LOOKS LIKE! (2x)

Martha:
I struggle with the gendered choices I have made, with a non-conventional career path that allowed me to focus on my two children. My scholarship focuses on feminist issues and I teach classes on gender, but I miss the days of action. It seems to me that many of my students have felt that the battle has been won, that feminism is no longer necessary or is even embarrassing. And yet, ironically,

the Republican war on women, which would roll back gains we have made and severely limit the control women have over their own bodies and lives, seems to have reawakened a sense of urgency. The opposite of feminism is complacency.

Together: FUCK COMPLACENCY!

Maggie:
After the strikes, I retreated into domesticity, teaching, and motherhood, losing myself in that ultimate, elusive love object: the tenure-track job. Take-to-the-streets activism seemed out of reach, but then there was BABEL: worlds collided, collectives were formed, real change began ...

Maggie: We are unstoppable ...
Martha: ... another world is possible!
Together: WE ARE UNSTOPPABLE, ANOTHER WORLD IS POSSIBLE!
Audience: WE ARE UNSTOPPABLE, ANOTHER WORLD IS POSSIBLE! (2x)

05/

BE CRITICAL!

Ruth Evans

I hate manifestos. They are so yesterday. Blast the manifesto! Its revolutionary impulse is, as James Simpson observes about a wholly different phenomenon and time period, to do with the desire for a clean break between then and now, a break in which the past is itself created "by being made very dark, wholly repellent, and sharply different from the brilliant new present."[1] I don't believe in the revolutionary break or the brilliant new present, although I'm with John Ball, that things have to change: "God doe bote, for now is time."[2] The

---

[1] James Simpson, "Making History Whole: Diachronic History and the Shortcomings of Medieval Studies," *Reading the Medieval in Early Modern England*, eds. David Matthews and Gordon McMullan (Cambridge, UK: Cambridge University Press, 2007), 21 [17–30].
[2] Letter of John Ball, from Stow's *Annales*, in *Medieval English Po-*

manifesto is always timely. So bless the manifesto! Whatever. I also hate the credo. I believe in things, but not in that absolute way.

I am going to make one point. Here's my manifesto: be critical! Clearly, critical is an overdetermined and loaded term. I will speak for English medieval studies, but other disciplines—philosophy, history, theology, cultural studies—understand different things by "critical," and it has meant different things historically (from its early modern sense of "given to censuring" to Kant's notion of distanciation). It is impossible to tease out its range of usages in my four minutes. Heidegger observes: "Most thought-provoking in our thought-provoking time is that we are still not thinking."[3] Deleuze urges that thought "has no other reason to *function than its own birth, always the repetition of its own birth*, secret and profound."[4] These are great manifestos but poor definitions of critical thinking. So where do we go?

Critical comes from "crisis" and was originally a medical term: to do with the crisis of a disease. To be critical is *not* to administer the remedy for a pathological crisis: rather, critique *happens* right where an illness might go either way—the patient will either decline or improve. To be critical is, in its origins, a matter of occupying a particular space (the body) and time (of crisis), and a matter (potentially) of life and death, perhaps of living on, of surviving (and I want medieval studies to survive). And it is an affair both of the body and the body politic: criticism comes from, and comes *with*, politics and affect—as long as we understand that affect is not only visceral but also a cultural construction.

Critical refers to the disciplinary norm of English. None of us wants to be *un*critical. But critical thinking is itself in crisis. On the one hand, we cry it up: we dutifully include statements in our syllabi that we plan to teach our students

---

lemical Writings, ed. James M. Dean, Middle English Texts Series (Kalamazoo: Medieval Institute Publications, 1996).
[3] Martin Heidegger, *What is Called Thinking?* trans. J. Glenn Gray (New York: Harper and Row, 1968), 6.
[4] Gilles Deleuze, *Cinema 2,* trans. Hugh Tomlinson and Robert Galeta (Minneapolis: University of Minnesota Press, 1989), 165.

"critical thinking," yet few of us explain what we mean by the term: it has become a pedagogical banality, revered as meaningful and yet utterly empty. Some waters here need serious muddying.[5]

On the other hand, critique (and here I am perhaps performing a dubious and uncritical slippage between related but different terms) is increasingly seen as something that academics and cultural theorists should abandon. Thus Graham Harman, in his 2002 book *Guerrilla Metaphysics*, advocates a style of philosophy that he calls "fascination"—in his words, "a kind of constructive thinking," one opposed to critical/analytical thought, though not to philosophical thinking.[6] Bruno Latour rails against critique—by which he means the various forms of demystificatory reading that came out of the Frankfurt School and that often goes under the rubric "critical theory—that is, a "dialectical critique of society," arguing that it has run out of steam, that it is self-satisfied and sterile, despite its cultural power: "The Zeus of Critique," says Latour, "rules absolutely, to be sure, but over a desert."[7] He wants a new kind of critic: "not the one who debunks, but the one who *assembles* ... , the one who offers the participants arenas in which to *gather*."[8] For Latour (and I cannot do justice here to his subtle argument), critique's relentless negativity, its iconoclasm, does not make anything new: "*what performs a critique*," he says in the "Compositionist Manifesto," "*cannot also compose*."[9] Critique does not generate anything. It comes to a full stop.

The calls to re-examine critical practice in the humani-

---

[5] See further Michael Warner, "Uncritical Reading," *Polemic: Critical or Uncritical*, ed. Jane Gallop (New York: Routledge, 2004), 13–38, and Amy Hollywood, "Reading as Self-Annihilation," in *Polemic*, ed. Gallop, 39–63.
[6] Graham Harman, *Guerrilla Metaphysics: Phenomenonology and the Carpentry of Things* (Chicago: Open Court Publishing, 2005), x.
[7] Bruno Latour, "Why Has Critique Run out of Steam?" *Critical Inquiry* 30 (2004): 239 [225–248].
[8] Latour, "Why Has Critique Run out of Steam?" 246, emphasis mine.
[9] Bruno Latour, "An Attempt at a 'Compositionist' Manifesto," *New Literary History* 41 (2010): 246 [471–490].

ties are also taking place within English: think of Eve Sedgwick's proposal that we replace "paranoid' reading with "reparative reading,"[10] or the opposition identified by Sharon Marcus and Stephen Best between surface vs. symptomatic reading.[11]

This debate is way too polarized. Is the only choice that between debunking or fascination? Demystification or description? Critical distance or textual attachment? Paranoia or love? Over thirty years ago, Tom Shippey offered his diagnosis of the crisis of health in the body politic of medieval scholarship as one caused by the rush to publish in nonspecialist journals because of the pressure of tenure. This rush, he argues, exhibits, in his words, "a lack of the eighteenth-century quality 'candour,'" by which he means, above all, "the desire to see difficult issues cleared up without the introduction of debating points."[12] He continues: "The urge to have as many 'publications' as possible is fatal to candour," fatal, that is to one's sense of having reservations about an argument or a methodology. The perverse effects of this, he argues, include "a new definition of 'scholarship' as 'familiarity with secondary material' [and here I'm mindful of Bill Readings' observation that "mere antiquarian erudition is not *critical*"][13] and [to continue with Shippey] a promotion of boldness over honest doubt." I read Shippey's "candour" and "doubt" here as versions of "critical," even as I recognize that his terms are relatively unnuanced and I do not believe in the notion of the disinterested critic. But Shippey goes on to make a crucial point that is still highly relevant today: "learned literary journals ... do not open texts up for other readers, they do not generate delight in literature."

---

[10] Eve Kosofsky Sedgwick, "Paranoid Reading and Reparative Reading, or, You're So Paranoid, You Probably Think This Essay Is About You," in Eve Kosofsky Sedgwick, *Touching Feeling: Affect, Pedagogy, Performativity* (Durham: Duke University Press: 2003), 123–152.

[11] Stephen Best and Sharon Marcus, "Surface Reading: An Introduction," *Representations* 108 (2009): 1–21.

[12] Tom Shippey, "Medievalia and Market Forces," *Times Literary Supplement,* June 6, 1980: 647.

[13] Bill Readings, *The University in Ruins* (Cambridge, MA: Harvard University Press, 1996), 81.

Shippey and Latour make odd bedfellows, and have utterly different perspectives, but at stake for both is the notion of what reading—criticism—is *for*—and how best to do it.

The problem Shippey identified in 1980—the professionalization of the discipline and its impact on the analysis of our pleasure in reading texts—has been both amplified and changed. The explosion of internet reading and writing—blogging, online journals, reviews, and comments—has transformed the field of medieval studies: it has massively increased the critical conversation (for the better) and changed the rhythm of that conversation (in ways that we have scarcely begun to analyze), although arguably—given the relentless professional drive to demonstrate scholarly "impact" in terms of the perceived quality of the places where one publishes—it still leaves open the question of the extent to which these alternative venues for publication and critique are supplementary or complementary to learned journals.

We need to acknowledge the absolute strangeness of medieval texts—and also the ways in which they are mute before our gaze. But we need more, not less, critique, and more, not less, historicizing, to explain these phenomena. We need to understand and analyze how those texts move us and why they continue to delight and surprise us, and for this we need to develop the critical tools that will allow us to analyze our bafflement and our passions.

06/

THIS IS YOUR BRAIN ON MEDIEVAL STUDIES

Joshua R. Eyler

The time has come to vigorously fight back against the devaluation of the humanities by policy makers and by college administrations that seek to close programs due to so-called financial exigencies, and I believe that Medieval Studies has an important role to play in this battle. Part of me thinks that, out of mere principle, we should refuse to kowtow to these threats and to hold our line that the humanities are inherently valuable in and of themselves; after all, they have served as the foundation for a university education for centuries. In the end, though, my more pragmatic side wins out. The push for accountability will not slacken, but will steadily increase, as we move into the future.

To win the fight we must do more than talk about

why the humanities are *important*. Yes, they help students to develop critical thinking skills; they allow us to solve problems or communicate in better ways; they contribute to an appreciation of our world, our culture, our differences, our democracy, ourselves. You can insert here any of the numerous defenses people have made. All of these points are true, but this line of reasoning is not working. Until we can prove that the humanities are *necessary*, as opposed to simply significant, for our universities and our students, we will continue to lose the rhetorical and financial struggle, and our resources will go to those fields that have done a better job than we have at proving why they are essential. But how do we do this? I suggest that we turn to the brain.

Brain-based learning theories, which lie at the intersection of cognitive neuroscience and the scholarship of teaching and learning, have made tremendous gains in articulating what physically happens in students' brains when they learn. Using this methodology, I have begun a project to try to show that the humanities profoundly and permanently affect the structures of students' brains in a way that is different from other fields and, thus, these modes of inquiry cannot be replaced. For example, we now know that in order to access prior knowledge and to use this knowledge to create new neuronal networks (otherwise known as learning), our brains weave concrete bits of information into stories and metaphors.[1] It stands to reason, then, that fields where we teach our students to work with written, visual, or musical narratives will help their brains to more easily create the mechanisms for making meaning. As an interdisciplinary field, Medieval Studies is well positioned to contribute to our knowledge here, if we take advantage of the multiple kinds of narratives embedded in our field to study how our students are learning.

More than this, though, Medieval Studies frequently

---

[1] See James E. Zull, *The Art of Changing the Brain: Enriching the Practice of Teaching by Exploring the Biology of Learning* (Sterling, VA: Stylus, 2002).

presents students with what I call "narratives of alterity," where they must wrestle with a variety of ideas that are different from and often clash with each other. Think of all the different languages, ideologies, cultures, etc., about which students must learn in our classes. Now, not only are they developing the cognitive pathways for new knowledge, but they must also create more neuronal networks in order to reconcile what the brain perceives as conflicting elements of information. In short, if we can somehow show that the humanities are not just useful, but also elemental, vital, and necessary, for the development of our students' brains and cognitive processes, we might be able to swing the momentum of the battle back towards us a bit.

The relevance doesn't stop with this political argument, either. In general, Medieval Studies can teach us more about how students learn. To what extent, for instance, can the difficulties students have with learning Middle English be attributed to the amygdala, which is one of the primary areas of the brain that controls conditioned and unconditioned fear responses? As teachers, then, if we learn some basic techniques for lessening amygdalar activity, will students have an easier time learning Chaucer? These are experiments that need to happen. So let's collaborate with colleagues in our biology and psychology departments, and in our centers for teaching and learning, and begin to map the undiscovered territory of the brain.

07/

STICKING TOGETHER

Lara Farina

If I'm going into the future, I want the things I've read to come along. Not that I have much choice; they'll stick with me, anyway. Many of them have doubtless stuck with you, too. They may have stuck us together, you and I. And they're always nudging us for further introductions—to students, colleagues, friends, readers, lovers, anyone, really, who will invite them to parties and workshops and conversations of all kinds. We shouldn't begrudge this promiscuous behavior, since time spent with others does not require that they spend less with us. That's one of their special charms, this temporal non-economy, this unhinging of time from trade.

Let's begin with a favorite, shall we? We may as well, because it's here with us, anyway. You know the story about the couple that gets stuck together? I'm sure you do. Let me (re)introduce you to my version:

> *Richere, a merchant (yes, I know, a merchant whose name is basically "rich guy," not exactly subtle, but stick with me) ... anyway, Richere, who is in some kind of legal or business trouble, receives shelter at a monastery where the abbot gives him a room not too far from the community's church. Stuck there with the monks, Richere sends for his wife. When she arrives, she and he have sex. We would think this would be fine, they being married and the sex being uninteresting enough to avoid any pointed description, but God is touchier about these things than we are. Richere and wife were "too nigh" the church for God's liking—not in the church, not on the altar or anything wild like that, just close enough. Close enough that God is mighty displeased, and the Mr. and Mrs. find themselves stuck together. Stuck together like "dog and bitch," moreover (which, so I'm told, is a pretty unpleasant thing). They yell for help. The brothers come running (and probably snickering, we would imagine). After getting the Richeres to promise to provide the monastery with support in years to come, the brothers pray for them, and they are released. Everyone is so impressed by this miracle that the abbot has it written down so that it will stick around forever.*

The story is filled with macabre humor, but the tale's staying power is no joke. Circulated in various forms and contexts from late antiquity onward, the narrative has the adhesive quality of an urban legend.[1] The version above, which is the one that lives with me, the one I can recall with no need to reference a printed edition, is based on Robert Mannyng's 1303 confessor's manual, *Handlyng*

---

[1] See Dyan Elliot, *Fallen Bodies: Pollution, Sexuality, and Demonology in the Middle Ages* (Philadelphia: University of Pennsylvania Press, 1999), 61–80.

Synne.[2] My first encounter with Mannyng was in an anthology of medieval literature, in which the Richere story, together with that other story about sticking, "The Dancers of Colbek" (you doubtless know this one too), was offered as a representative exemplum. I'm guessing that this was also your experience, since these two tales—the sticky ones—are mostly what we stick to when we read or talk about *Handlyng Synne*.

Why do we stick to them? Current scholarship is not very well poised to answer this question. That we *do* stick to them is even something of an embarrassment. By doing so, we slyly refuse to give the larger textual context its expected dues, limiting how we can use the stories to talk about historical subjects like the institution of confession, Mannyng's relation to his source texts, the intended audience for the work, and so forth. Such willful selection of the juicy bits of Mannyng's manual is, by our own current standards, unwise, yet we stick to it anyway. Still, we can feel the weight of the profession bear down on us when we read the requisite rationales for writing, yet again, about the only parts that anyone ever writes about: *"Although much discussed already, the Richere story is particularly useful for examining ..."; "The Dancers of Colbek exemplum is worth revisiting for ..."*[3] I myself was going to offer one such justification, claiming the tale's utility for a timely manifesto. But this is a time *to manifest*, to play, festively, with the hands we are dealt. So—fuck it—fuck me—I'm (re)telling you the story because it sticks with us.

We can imagine why medieval religious like the monks portrayed in the tale would stick to the Richere story, since it would be useful for highlighting their authority vis-à-vis the laity. We can imagine why Mannyng

---

[2] Robert Mannyng, *Handlyng Synne*, ed. Idelle Sullens (Binghamton: MRTS, 1983). Both the Richere story and the "Dancers of Colbek" are from the section on sacrilege: ll. 8941–8990 and ll. 8991–9257, respectively.

[3] Since I hear these as imperatives of our profession, these are paraphrases, not quotes from particular analyses.

would stick it in his manual; its usefulness takes a nifty twist when Mannyng turns the tables on the would-be-confessor reader by asserting that he shouldn't feel so superior to the Richeres since the clerical habit of fucking other men's wives is so much worse (who's snickering now, priest-man?). We can imagine ourselves making use of these exemplum—to talk about power, authority, history, form, and language. Can we imagine ourselves stuck? We are not supposed to like sticking. Nor are we expected to like stories about sticking. The critical consensus on *Handlyng Synne* is that it is a terrorizing, or at least shaming, work, one that returns us to our fallen state, refusing to offer a durable "cure" for our transgressions. These interpretations require that we be horrified at the imagination of being glued together like dog and bitch (for we've all heard that is a pretty unpleasant thing). If we take any pleasure in imagining ourselves fixed like the Richeres, the butt of this joke, we're fucked. We are *used*, not *using* for acceptable purposes.[4]

Psychoanalytic theory of course offers an explanation of a (fucked-up) desire to stick to things like this. In his essay on "The Uncanny," Freud proposes that we seize upon unwanted repetition (i.e., experiences of finding oneself back in the same place or situation) because these occasions can respond to a repetition-compulsion that lies deep at the core of our instincts. He hypothesizes that we

---

[4] In addition to Elliot, see: Mark Miller, "Displaced Souls, Idle Talk, Spectacular Scenes: *Handlyng Synne* and the Perspective of Agency" *Speculum* 71.3 (1996): 606–632; Andrew J. Power, "Telling Tales in Robert Mannyng de Brun's *Handlyng synne*," in *The Ghost Story from the Middle Ages to the Twentieth Century*, eds. Helen Conrad O'Briain and Julie Anne Stevens (Dublin: Four Courts, 2010), 34–46; and Robert J. Hasenfratz, "Terror and Pastoral Care in *Handlyng Synne*," in *Texts and Traditions of Medieval Pastoral Care*, eds. Catherine Gunn and Catherine Innes-Parker (York, UK: York Medieval Press, 2009), 132–148, for discussion of *Handlyng Synne*'s use of shame and horror. I am not arguing here that a view of *Handlyng Synne* as terrorizing is unwarranted. Mannyng himself states his intent to scare his audience with the Dancers of Colbek story (ll. 9254–9255).

desire a return to undifferentiated, intra-uterine experience, but that each time we reimagine this experience, the specter of separation/castration chases us away.[5] Thus, we get stuck in a circle of pleasure and horror. As analysts, we may not want, now, to stick to Oedipus anymore. But Freud's discussion of the uncanny *does* fit Mannyng's exempla like a glove fits a hand—or like a bitch fits a dog. It fits so well it is itself uncanny. Filled with independently acting body parts, doubling and repetition, and genitals that may never come back, "Richere" and "Colbek" seem the exact prequel to the examples of the uncanny Freud cites. The father of psychoanalysis even offers a Mannyng-like exemplum of his own, in which he details his rising dread at finding himself repeatedly returning to a bad part of town despite his efforts to leave.[6]

We might also stick with "The Uncanny" because it concerns literary aesthetics and why we like to read stories about being stuck (and isn't it the critic's job to ask why?). Yet, fittingly for a discussion of what it feels like to get nowhere, Freud offers no explanation that lets us be done with the question and move on. Instead, he ends his essay by summoning literature's affective power, putting himself back into the experience of reading:

> ... the story-teller has a peculiarly directive influence over us; by means of the states of mind into which he can put us and the expectations he can rouse in us, he is able to guide the current of our emotions, dam it up in one direction and make it flow in another, and he often obtains a great variety of effects from the same material. All this is nothing new, and has doubtless long since been fully taken into account by professors of aesthetics. We have drifted into this field of research half

---

[5] See Sigmund Freud, *Collected Papers, Vol. 4*, International Psycho-Analytical Library, no. 10, ed. Ernest Jones (New York: Basic Books, 1959), 368–407.

[6] Freud, *Collected Papers,* 389–390.

involuntarily, through the temptation to explain certain instances which contradicted our theory ...[7]

"All this is nothing new"—this is not analysis but affirmation. Overcome with feeling, Freud lets go of argument and its imperative to make progress. He lets himself drift, half involuntarily, back to his own pleasure, which is our pleasure too, the pleasure of being stuck with a story about being stuck. He lets someone else take charge of his currents and flows. He's fucked.

If we're fucked, we can be fucked together through the things that we read. This is not as bad as it may sound to you. It's certainly better than the alternative of sticking to stories so we can feel ourselves superior to the characters, the author, the book, the culture, or the period. That is an act of separation we can do without. Those of us stuck to the Middle Ages get quite enough of the smugness that comes with narratives of cultural progress already. Rather, let us feel ourselves sticking to the Richeres and to the dancers, to Mannyng and even to Freud as he circles in confusion back to the bad part of town.

Having been there before us, and before the father of psychoanalysis too, *Handlyng Synne* offers us a feel for the pleasures of sticking. In his prologue, Mannyng asks that his readers handle his book often, noting that it need not be read in order, for wherever the reader opens it, or however the pages are turned, we will find ourselves at the beginning.[8] His desire for a repetitive handling of his book, with its promise of lasting accommodation (it can begin wherever you want, whenever you want, and it is always beginning), offers the unceasing caress as readerly delight. This is a sticking of body to text that does not need to move on to avoid boredom or panic. And, yes, the sticking returns us to sin, but Mannyng is well aware that sin is fun; that reading about sin is fun; and that reading about sin is to imaginatively participate in sin, which is

---

[7] Freud, *Collected Papers*, 406.
[8] *Handlyng Synne*, ll. 82–146.

both fun and sinful. By handling sin, we are going nowhere, but these are pleasures that won't be depleted if we linger.

If we stick to the very moment(s) of sticking in the Richere story, we can imagine a non-teleological pleasure. Pleasure out of sequential time is either paradisal or perverse (or perhaps both). The stuck fuck, though it does end in one way, conjures the possibility of a deeply queer being in time: why should we end a good thing? What if the Richeres didn't yell for the (possibly snickering) monks? What if we choose to ignore the sense that it is time to get back to work or business or the proper life of the laity; time to back off for the sake of production and reproduction? Then we have pleasure that eschews release. We may also have an ethics of sticking together.

Our profession, with its sharply defined levels of achievement, has its own horror stories about getting stuck. We talk about the obsessive who can't seem to write about more than one text, the endless reviser, the doctoral student who will never finish the dissertation, the Assistant Professor with the 4/4 teaching load who will never be able to "write her way out," and the defeated Associate who has given up on making it to Full. We hope we don't stall out like these pitiable figures. As a teacher of graduate students, I occasionally encounter the rare person who is taking classes for personal satisfaction and not to move into a career in academia. We might celebrate such passion, but instead we (other students, colleagues, and myself) are often profoundly disturbed by the presence of people spending so much time and money for "nothing." We could stand to remove some of these fears—fears that divide us from each other—by reconceiving what it is to be stuck.

The stories that stick with us are standing by, ready to help in this endeavor, and not just by leading us to new ideas about how we spend time or progress. Reading is affective practice. When we read or recall what we read, we practice the feeling of return, repetition, and enmeshment. We practice being together with something or someone. Chaucer, having been there before us, writes about this all the time. His narrators' bedtime reading sticks with them and lets them stick by or to others. His poems stick disparate tales and tellers together for the pleasure of seeing what will happen. His more memorable pilgrims play with the possibility of endless prologue, of never getting to it or letting go.

I want a future in which we are not afraid to stick our favorite stories in places where they don't yet belong. A number of things can happen when they meet other texts; explanation of one by the other is only one of these things.[9] Let's aim for perverse pairings, so that we can feel what happens when they/we come together. Let's feel our way around this "we," this pronoun that is already like a party where the lights have gone out. Let's find out if we can forge new pleasures by feeling ourselves stuck.

---

[9] For inspiration, see the essays in *New Critical Modes*, ed. Jeffrey J. Cohen and Cary Howie, *postmedieval* 2.3 (2011).

08/

WAGING GUERRILLA WARFARE AGAINST THE 19TH CENTURY

Matthew Gabriele

The idea of writing a "manifesto" for this panel was particularly appealing to me for two reasons. First, I like being around people who work heavily in theory. Their perspectives and ideas continually challenge my own, even if, since I'm but a simple historian by training, I don't always understand what they're talking about. I implore my fellow panelists to therefore use small words so that I can follow along ...

Second, and more seriously, this panel became especially too good to pass up, in light of a recently rejected grant application to the NEH. Although generally positive in his/her comments, one reviewer said of my proposed project that Medieval Studies had no need of new methodologies. Now, there were caveats to this claim, but (to get to my point) this person's comment serves a useful purpose, since the whole point of a straw man is for there to be something to set alight. So, let me attempt (in my own modest way) to do just that. I don't intend to fire the straw man directly; let me instead try to torch the whole field. Part of the task of the scholar, as I see it, is to be daring. High risk, high reward, but also high rate of failure. If the straw man burns, so be it. If it singes me as well, so be it. Perhaps, looking around, the field's already on fire.

So, in the rest of this very brief mini-manifesto, let me try to set out the problem, and diagnose its causes. I hope there are suggestions in here somewhere. More likely, some in the audience will already have thought much about this and offer me help.

The problem I want to talk about is the tyranny of nineteenth- and early twentieth-century scholarship. The questions they asked of the period still define our work. We're still trapped, still stuck within their "textual community," trying to answer questions that are inherently teleological, always seeking answers to their end. We still seek to separate "religious" things and "secular" things. Nevermind that *religio* and *saeculum* had very different meanings than they do now. We still look at biblical citations through Protestant glasses, finding a verse from Jeremiah in an eleventh-century chronicle, and thinking "Jeremiah," when we should be thinking of the accreted weight of centuries of exegetical tradition. We still think in terms of nationalistic lineages in our literatures, as if the Anglo-Norman scribe of the Oxford *Roland* had Louis XIV in mind when he was writing; as if *Domesday* necessarily led to Henry VIII.

Part of the reason for this disconnect has to do with the shape of the university. We still live in faculties created around the questions that animated our ancestors, subdivided into disciplines that made sense ca. 1900. We're created within this paradigm, live within it, progress, then produce others in our image. Not that there's anything wrong with that. In itself, it's a noble, artisanal pursuit. But we should, at least, acknowledge the paradigm exists. Its power comes from our tacit complicity.

So, instead of asking what more we can say about this or that source, instead of asking if we can know this or that event more accurately, perhaps we should first be asking other questions. After all, we know that Hugh Capet began a dynasty that would last for centuries, but he certainly didn't know there was a Philip the Fair in his future. For Hugh, the movement of time was contingent, uncertain, changeable. It isn't radical to say that looking backwards gives the illusion of narrative. This was as true for the ninth-century Franks as it is for us today. You see a path back to where you started and try to clear the accumulated brush. Yet, our subjects saw something different. They saw a field and a far distant goal. In that field, they walked, doubled-back, tried another way, and sometimes ended up far removed from where they intended. Our job is not only to find that path, but more importantly to find those footprints—all those footprints. And sometimes, for us to see those footprints, we shouldn't just clear the brush. Sometimes, we might need to set the whole field alight.

09/

MEDIEVAL STUDIES IN THE SUBJUNCTIVE MOOD

Gaelan Gilbert

> Life can only be understood backwards,
> but it must be lived forwards.
>
> Søren Kierkegaard

Let's just run with it. The potentially instructive, because utterly naïve, thought experiment of entertaining for a moment that we have never been modern. Forget modernism—what if *modernity* never happened? Not that we know what "modern" even means, except as an empty qualifier perched with pomp at the crest of history. Then again, that's precisely the point. Modernity, like Walter Benjamin's angel of history looking over its shoulder, has always been running from what it no longer wants to be, shouting "not that! not that!" And yet—and it's a big yet —if we are becoming increasingly convinced by Bruno

Latour, then not only were we never not medieval, but medieval no longer has to mean "premodern." If Benjamin's angel of modern history can't stop looking backward and defining itself in opposition to what it sees as a sort of *negative immanence* (what, in the past, it fears and loathes), then perhaps "to be medieval," as Andrew Cole and D. Vance Smith have put it, "is to posit a future in the very act of self-recognition, to offer a memory or memorial to a future that will be recognized at a time and place not yet known."[1] A future, that is, which positively transcends presence.

This isn't just another way of gesturing to what Maura Nolan (following Adorno) calls the "absent presence" of the medieval. In a stronger sense, we are and have always been *mid aevum,* amidst the ages that have been and those that will be, between the already and the not-yet, as Deleuzian theologians of the *eschaton* have put it.[2] Among them, St. Augustine reiterated the paradox of temporality by noting that the future doesn't exist except in the present, the future-present. And the psychological mode proper to the present? Attention. What to attend to? Why, to participating as much as possible in what we want (the future) *to become.* Which starts, has already started, now. As the Stagyrite said, since we are becoming and not yet being, there are traces of what we may be—but are not yet—in what we are now. Even Aquinas knew that existence precedes essence. Žižek said something similar recently, but with more utopian (as opposed to eschatological) intent: that only by treating certain critical signs of the present order as if they were signals from the future is revolution possible.[3] In any case, accounting

---

[1] Andrew Cole and D. Vance Smith, "Introduction: Outside Modernity," in Andrew Cole and D. Vance Smith, eds., *On the Legitimacy of the Middle Ages: On the Unwritten History of Theory* (Durham: Duke University Press, 2010), 19

[2] Christopher Ben Simpson, *Deleuze and Theology* (London: Bloomsbury, 2012).

[3] Slavoj Žižek, "Signs from the Future," lecture given in Zagreb, Croatia, May 14, 2012, and available at: https://www.youtube.com/watch?v=UrtcYq_wpho.

for Augustinian *temporal distension* is a tenuous position to find oneself in, because it is a position that one cannot construct, but must *find oneself in*. And this exciting fact abides: if time (and tensed language) is the house of Being, then we its inhabitants live and act in something like the subjunctive mood, with all the Heideggerian resonance of "mood" and its Anglo-Saxon source in *mod*, a mindful comportment or attentive disposition. Beyond and constitutive of subjectivity, is subjunctivity, the future conditional.

A medieval studies in the subjunctive mood would strive to articulate the ways in which medieval perspectives were hybrids of desirous hope for the not-yet and humble realism about the already-is, akin in more recent terms to a balance of Derrida's *avenir* and Harman's *allure*. Indeed, the *futurity of the medieval* has not been lost on certain moderns, whether in the artificial sublimity of Meillassoux's Tertullian-esque wagering on the impossible possibility of the birth of God or in the cultural halo of the Hegelian Spirit in Mannheim's delineation of heterodox chiliasm as the birth of utopia. In dealing with medieval futures, with what medieval persons and texts and agents wanted their future to become, moreover, we therefore deal weirdly with our own present, which is, after all, the (historical) fulfillment of the future of the medieval. It thus might be worth wondering whether we can strive paradoxically to move *forward with* medieval projections into the futures they imagined, the futures that ended up *becoming us*, and to do so as a way of grasping the *non-continuous contiguity* of historical periods. This admittedly demands some kind of folly-and-mystery-embracing leap on the part of the scholar, one that itself must be rigorously underwritten by a critical yet non-hypocritical naiveté (not unlike what Jane Bennett has recently called for in speculative orientation to non-humans). Yet wouldn't we be laughed off the stage if we asked how medieval anticipations of the future *overlapped* with our speculations about the past, like two arms folding over the lap of history's night? Or, following the lead of fantasy and science fiction writers like J.R.R.

Tolkien and Walter M. Miller, Jr. and political scientists like Jörg Friedrichs and Richard Ned Lebow, how they overlap with our own imagined futures?[4]

We probably would. Nonetheless, asking such naïve questions may be the first step toward a medieval studies in which the desire to relate with affective yet critical understanding to medieval pasts can quite simply merge with the delineation of medieval anticipations of future-presents that have intelligible but not reductive associations with our own. The aim is to cultivate something like empathy, or Stein's *Einfuhlung*, toward the past. After all, "no matter how rigorous our historicism, no matter how playful our post-structuralism, the Middle Ages remains both alien and familiar, total and local *at the same time*."[5] While what I'm trying to evoke here is nothing more than an ethos or comportment, in light of the inevitable complexity of any such problematizing gesture toward periodization, if we are serious about recognizing robust, tradition-grounded differences and contiguities within and between temporal multiplicities, then we are going to need determinate and recombinative narrative images of the medieval pasts that we are privileged and condemned ('destined' is too weak a word) to non-identically repeat.

So here, as a preliminary heuristic, are three general modes or moods of medieval subjunctivity, each of which styles futural contingency with varying degrees of prepa-

---

[4] See *Tolkien's Modern Middle Ages,* eds. Jane Chance and Alfred K. Siewers (New York: Palgrave MacMillan, 2009). For post-apocalyptic science fiction, see Walter M. Miller, Jr., *A Canticle for Leibowitz.* (Philadelphia: J.B. Lippincott & Co., 1960). For neomedievalist international relations theory, see Jörg Friedrichs, *European Approaches to International Relations Theory* (London: Routledge, 2007), especially chap. 7, "The Meaning of New Medievalism: An Exercise in Theoretical Reconstruction," 127–145. For the use of counterfactuals in political science, see Richard Ned Lebow, *Forbidden Fruit: Counterfactuals and International Relations* (Princeton: Princeton University Press, 2010).

[5] Maura Nolan, "Making the Aesthetic Turn: Adorno, the Medieval, and the Future of the Past," *Journal of Medieval and Early Modern Studies* 34.3 (Fall 2004): 570 [549–575].

ration, resistance, or openness:

I. (Religious) Imminence: Apocalypse or Death Comportment: *the future as an approaching, ineluctable actant*
II. (Chivalric-Economic) Adventure: The Pursuit of Happiness Comportment: *the future as risky yet profitably opportune actant*
III. (Political) Prudence: Struggling with Fortune Comportment: *the future as a dangerous yet strategically manageable actant*

These comportments and the details of their diegetic unfolding can offer a productive milieu, I think, for close (phenomenological) and distant (structuralist) readings of contingency and temporal distension. Methodological hazards aside, it is important to become increasingly sensitive to the ways our cultural institutions and affairs are partial fulfillments and betrayals of the hopes, plans, or fears of medieval thinkers, because doing so can thicken our tactical repertoires for not only surviving but also thriving in the academy, especially in the face of the exigencies of humanities education today. The academy, including the impactful assemblages of classroom and publishing, is a site for the enactment of an attentive psychological mode proper to the past-present: "recollection." To "recollect" is: 1) to assemble and reassemble for purposes of dialogue in a common material location (even if disseminated via digital technologies), and, for the humanities, and, 2) to engage at such assemblies in the comported remembrance and exploration of that which according to the logic of global capitalism is deemed utterly valueless, in part because it can offer such acute vantages on present intentionality: the past. A truly democratic culture, after all, must insist that a voice be extended, as Chesterton suggested, to the dead. Through recollection, medieval studies can teach modernity how to appreciate its post-medieval obligations without slipping into historical Darwinism.[6] So let's dare to see potential not only in medieval studies' methodological apparatus but also in its unique mixture of institutional materiality (of codicology, building code, and digital code), potential for tempering the field's charming dustiness (as the public sees) with a commitment to itinerant forms of dialogue, publication, credentialing, and pedagogy, not least as a political *counter-response* to our field's nationalistic origins. Collaboration and anonymity, familiar to pedagogy but still foreign to textual research, will need to take on important new roles. But we'll also have to extend our aims beyond the academy, where, suffice it to say, we have friends whose contributions will be invaluable. So where, you may ask, are all these new St. Benedicts capable of participating in and organizing para-academic networks of hospitality, intellectual labor, apprenticeship, public debate, and philological community? (Look in the mirror.) One early step will be for academics and para-academics to adopt a readiness—which, as Hamlet rightly insists, "is all" (5.2.223)—to inquire into a topic which it is long since time to broach: namely, what it might mean to have wanted and then rejected a cenobitic form-of-life beyond the biopolitical parameters of instrumental capital.[7] The question of the hour to come, in other words, if we are talking about medieval studies as a network of material collectives and imperatives, will have to do with how the vestiges of the European monastic fragmentation, a lacuna eventually filled by the modern multiversity and a central factor for understanding the latter's predicament, have always remained with us, are us, the unceasing dissolution of the humanities.

---

[6] See Nicholas Watson. "The Phantasmal Past: Time, History, and the Recombinative Imagination," *Studies in the Age of Chaucer* 32 (2012): 1–37.
[7] Giorgio Agamben, *The Highest Poverty: Monastic Rules and Form-of-Life* (Stanford: Stanford University Press, 2013).

10/

RADICAL RIDICULE

Noah D. Guynn

We've been hearing a lot lately about the "descriptive turn" in literary studies, which is as much a turn away from critical hermeneutics and symptomatic reading as a turn toward observation and description. This isn't a neutral development or a mere change in direction. On the contrary, it entails a broad-based repudiation of Marxism, psychoanalysis, and post-structuralism as methodologies that are unconsciously enmeshed in the very humanist ideologies they purport to demystify. It also frequently trips over its own feet, formulating critiques of critique in order supposedly to move beyond it.

Thus Heather Love seeks to challenge Paul Ricoeur's hermeneutics of suspicion, arguing that he exposes belief as false consciousness even as he prophesies redemption through exegesis, "clear[ing] the horizon," as he puts it, "for a more authentic word, for a new reign of Truth."[1] Noting a perennial tension between demystification and restoration in contemporary criticism, Love urges us to consider how to make "a significant departure from the humanist underpinnings of traditional close reading" (387). Specifically, she proposes that we emulate the methods of antihumanist sociologists like Bruno Latour and Erving Goffman, scholars who understand the social domain as flat and thin rather than deep and thick and who seek "the real variety that is already there" rather than the underlying ideologies that can "explain the world" (377). At the same time, Love must acknowledge how difficult such a departure will be: Ricoeur's messianic longing is "in our institutional DNA, in the 'art of interpreting' that still defines us" (388). Indeed, the rhetoric of the descriptive turn contains an aporia: by unveiling the humanist ideology at the heart of ideological unveiling, Love constructs a dialectic that, like Ricoeur's, seeks to transcend itself.

A similar problem is right on the surface of Stephen Best and Sharon Marcus's introduction to "surface reading," which opens with a bold critique of Frederic Jamesons's claim that critique is capable of revealing the deep, latent, ideological meanings concealed beneath literal, manifest, literary ones. Far from achieving political emancipation, they argue, symptomatic reading instead emulates Christian, or more precisely Gnostic, theories of recessive truth, linking "the power of the critic with that of the God of biblical hermeneutics, who can transcend the blinkered point of view of humankind."[2] They call for a turn away from this "heroic" (15), indeed messianic conception of the critic and toward the supposedly more transparent, "relatively neutral" (16), and politically "real-

---

[1] Paul Ricoeur, *Freud and Philosophy: An Essay on Interpretation*, trans. Denis Savage (New Haven: Yale University Press, 1970), 33, cited in Heather Love, "Close but not Deep: Literary Ethics and the Descriptive Turn," *New Literary History* 41.2 (2010): 388 [371–92]; hereafter cited parenthetically in text.

[2] Stephen Best and Sharon Marcus, "Surface Reading: An Introduction," *Representations* 108.1 (2009): 15 [1–21].

ist" methodologies (15) that "attend to the surfaces of texts rather than plumb their depths" (1–2). A variety of hermeneutic procedures fall under this rubric: new formalism, history of the book, cognitive reading, reparative reading, immanent reading, distant reading, *just* reading, and so on. All look for "what is evident, perceptible, apprehensible in texts ... what insists on being looked *at* rather than what we must train ourselves to see *through*" (9). Of course it's hard to overlook the fact that Best and Marcus legitimize the move beyond symptomatic reading through a diagnosis of Jameson's hero syndrome and God complex, or that their heralding of a transformation in critical practices shares some of the evangelical fervor it decries.

Though it is sorely tempting, I will not respond to the descriptive turn by perversely intoning the mantras of Ricoeur's Holy Trinity (Marx, Nietzsche, Freud), or by dismissing the repudiation of critique as false consciousness, *ressentiment,* or a return of the repressed.[3] Instead, I will focus on some of the original, positive moves Love, Best and Marcus, and other surface readers make—moves that may hold real appeal for politically engaged scholars of the medieval past.

To begin with, let me say I think it's a fantastic idea to revitalize literary studies by adopting social science methods like those of Latour and Goffman. Another possible source of inspiration from this realm is James C. Scott, whose political anthropology is strongly descriptive but who doesn't eschew the explanatory force of latency and depth. On the contrary, Scott concentrates on both the "public" and "hidden" transcripts of social exchange, noting that the latter (which he also calls "infrapolitics") may be difficult to track using purely empirical methods but can nonetheless be retrieved and described. His particular interest is in subaltern groups, which are highly constrained in power-laden situations but have an "imag-

---

[3] Ricoeur: "Three masters, seemingly mutually exclusive, dominate the school of suspicion: Marx, Nietzsche, and Freud" (*Freud and Philosophy,* 32).

inative capacity ... to reverse or negate dominant ideologies" using discreet gestures, veiled language, and low-profile tactics.[4]

Scott's approach is especially fruitful when it comes to the analysis of medieval Carnival, its topsy-turvy forms of social ridicule, and the various performance genres associated with it: farce, *sottie, Fastnachtspiele,* mumming, and so on.[5] According to Terry Eagleton's classic Marxian critique, Carnival is "a *licensed* affair in every sense, a permissible rupture of hegemony, a contained popular blow-off, as disturbing and relatively ineffectual as a revolutionary work of art. As Shakespeare's Olivia remarks, there is no slander in an allowed fool."[6] Disavowing Carnival's manifest if ritualized forms of political

---

[4] James C. Scott, *Domination and the Arts of Resistance: Hidden Transcripts* (New Haven: Yale University Press, 1990), 91; hereafter cited parenthetically in text. Scott's work is filled with literary references and theatrical metaphors, and has been especially influential in the field of performance studies. See, inter alia, L.M. Bogad, *Electoral Guerrilla Theatre: Radical Ridicule and Social Movements* (New York: Routledge, 2005), from which I borrowed the title for this manifesto.

[5] For a pan-European perspective on Carnival drama, see Konrad Eisenbichler and Wim N.M. Hüsken, *Carnival and the Carnivalesque: The Fool, the Reformer, the Wildman, and Others in Early Modern Theater* (Amsterdam: Rodopi, 1999). I am currently writing a book that seeks out hidden transcripts in early French drama: *The Many Faces of Farce: Ethics, Politics, and Urban Culture in Medieval and Early Modern France.*

[6] Terry Eagleton, *Walter Benjamin, or Towards a Revolutionary Criticism* (New York: Verso, 1981), 148, citing *Twelfth Night* 1.5.90. As Barbara A. Babcock notes, Marx himself viewed ritual rebellion "as a significant step in the development of a revolutionary class consciousness." Trotsky's view has tended to prevail among cultural critics, however, especially those who reject Mikhail Bakhtin's nostalgic, utopian conception of Carnival. Like Eagleton, Trotsky regarded seasonal festivals as a means for "preserving the established order and thereby hindering the emergence of a revolutionary consciousness." See Barbara A. Babcock, "Introduction," in *The Reversible World: Symbolic Inversion in Art and Society,* ed. Barbara A. Babcock (Ithaca: Cornell University Press, 1972), 22.

subversion, Eagleton interprets it as an ideological ploy used to contain the very resistance it superficially allows. Much like a surface reader, Scott counters that this sort of functionalist reading of Carnival mistakenly "ascribes a unique agency to elites" (178) and wrongly assumes that subalterns are benighted by ideology to the point of being incapable of real, sustained resistance.

In fact, as ethnographers and social psychologists have amply demonstrated, subalterns may be "*less* constrained at the level of thought and ideology, since they can in secluded settings speak with comparative safety, and *more* constrained at the level of political action and struggle, where the daily exercise of power sharply limits the options available to them" (91). If Carnival is "a ritual modeling of revolt," Scott asks polemically, might it not also "serve as a dress rehearsal or a provocation for *actual* defiance," which may or may not include *visible* defiance (178)? Drawing on celebrated histories of Carnival that Eagleton simply overlooks,[7] Scott argues that recessive discourses and actions are real historical phenomena even if they fail to register in a purely empirical observation of the past.

Which leads me to my own polemical question: Might the descriptive turn point us in the direction of a return to history and reinvigorated, more highly nuanced modes of historicist critique? Far from matching texts to flat, static contexts, a *new* New Historicism might examine instead what Paul Strohm has called "the unruly multiplicity of ways in which history can manifest itself within a text."[8] Many of the vestiges of history are visible on the surface of texts. Pace Eagleton, we should include here the forms of hegemonic rupture characteristic of Carnival, a feast of misrule that has been too quickly do-

---

[7] See, for example, Emmanuel Le Roy Ladurie, *Carnival in Romans,* trans. Mary Feeney (New York: George Braziller, 1979), and Yves-Marie Bercé, *Fêtes et révolte: Des mentalités populaires du XVIe au XVIIIe siècles* (Paris: Hachette, 1976).

[8] Paul Strohm, "Historicity without Historicism?" *postmedieval* 1.3 (2010): 382 [380–391].

mesticated in the name of critical suspicion. Other remnants of history lurk beneath the surface of texts and point mutely or indirectly to hidden transcripts. This includes practices of cultural resistance and political insubordination that were never meant to be seen, but nonetheless existed in utterly pervasive ways. These social forces are well worth recovering, if only so that we can offer a more nuanced picture of the diversity of human experience and the complexity of social exchange in the medieval past.

11/

BURN(ED) BEFORE WRITING:
THE LATE STAGES OF A LATE MEDIEVAL PHD
AND CURRENT ACADEMIC REALITIES

David Hadbawnik

SCENE ONE

Facebook friend Jeffrey Jerome Cohen posts the following remark on September 13, 2011:

> The JIL [Job Information List of the Modern Language Association] is out today, and it looks to be another grim year for jobs in medieval and early modern studies. Best wishes for all who are on the market.

This draws a number of comments from chagrined job-seekers and faculty in short-handed departments.

SCENE TWO

On September 15, Jim, one of the numerous assistant VPs in the research office where I am employed in a public Research I university, shoots me a little look as he explains that I'm to proofread the proposal he just e-mailed me, which is due tomorrow. A typical example of the language of the proposal is as follows:

> The lowest transverse-electric (TE_1) mode of the PPWG can exhibit intrinsic (ohmic) losses in the dB/km range, when it is over-moded. Furthermore, it should be possible to excite this mode exclusively, by careful mode-matching at the input facet. Additional calculations indicate that diffractive losses [...] To be successful and ultimately attain financial self-sufficiency, the NERC will work to (i) **engage industry and the business world in the highest-level interaction by minimizing the above uncertainties**, and (ii) **incorporate future needs** (markets) **for NERC products** in the evolving focus of the Center. The exposure of Center students and faculty to industrial needs (so-called **market pull**) will produce engineering graduates with the depth and breadth of education needed for success in technological innovation, and for effective future career leadership.

I realize that the style of this proposal—with its mixture of scientific and business jargon, its seemingly random use of font features to emphasize esoteric terms, its use of unexplained acronyms—constitutes a genre completely foreign to the discourse of humanities (which, of course, has its own jargon). But what had never struck me before was how the very messiness of it, its seemingly needless convolutions, signals something important, contained in the little look Jim gave me in his office: "*We're too busy to worry about proper grammar and formatting conventions ... we're inventing stuff and making money.*" This attitude, in light of the hardships apparent across all academic disciplines, demands a grudging respect, even if I ultimately don't agree with it.

SCENE THREE

That same day, in a graduate seminar, we are looking at Robert Pogue Harrison's amazing book *Forests*, and the professor tells us, "This is one of my favorite books, but it's a book you absolutely can't write today." He explains that the wide range of texts and periods covered by Harrison—everything from *Gilgamesh* to Dante to Joseph Conrad—would simply appear too eclectic on the job market. I am often told things like this, even as I'm also told that to survive, the humanities must become more "interdisciplinary," which seems a contradiction. Taken altogether with the above scenes, how can we begin to reconcile these messages for those hoping to complete their first projects and begin looking for a job?

With this in mind, I want to briefly outline three concrete suggestions for expanding the discipline, while encouraging students to maintain a sense of adventure in their projects that might actually help rather than limit their opportunities on the job market.

Embrace theory.

Traditional medieval studies has regarded theory with suspicion, and indeed, an overreliance on theory or following trends too slavishly can make one appear to lack "rigor." But psychoanalysis is perfect for exploring medieval romance (and vice-versa); Object-Oriented Ontology has proven fruitful in rethinking the materiality of and in medieval objects and texts; biopolitics and ecocriticism can provide insights into the development of power and partitioning of land and sea during the medieval and early modern periods. Moreover, departments increasingly seek candidates who can talk and teach theory in combination with a traditional period in the discipline. As the recent announcement of four tenure-track positions in Transgender Studies at Arizona State University over the next two years suggests, the demand for versatility in such backgrounds will only continue to grow.

Get creative.

Medieval conferences often include panels on the fiction of J.R.R. Tolkien, J.K. Rowling, and George R.R. Martin, but as a new generation of medievalists who also have MFAs emerges, there are no programs I know of that offer period-informed approaches to creative writing; usually, students in such classes are discouraged from so-called "genre" writing because it is not literary enough. Yet creative writing is one of the few "growth areas" in English departments, and popular medieval-inflected fiction is in large part what drives that interest. A highly popular course taught by Tim Machan at Marquette University, which houses a large Tolkien archive, addresses the creative and scholarly sides of Tolkien's work. More could be done—imagine a hybrid course that combines serious medieval literary scholarship with creative assignments. Such a course would tap in to the demand for creative writing while expanding interest in medieval studies.

Go digital.

Like theory, Digital Humanities is a contentious term, with even some forward-thinking medievalists suggesting it's a fad not worth pursuing. They couldn't be more wrong. For one thing, digitization means democratization in research. There is an urgent need for rare texts to be made available to more scholars and the broader public. Such work is precisely the kind of project that VPs like Jim in my research office would recognize and reward; indeed, the Tesserae project (a digital search engine that compares Classical texts for allusions), developed at University at Buffalo, has drawn National Endowment for the Humanities research dollars to the school. Similarly, Dorothy Kim is co-leading the Archive of Early Middle English project, which will create a searchable database of severely understudied manuscripts, with encoded information on names, places, intertextual elements, philological, paleographical and material features—opening the texts to a much broader range of scholars with new analytical tools offered by technology. Such projects also provide students with the opportunity to get in on the ground floor of important new research, co-authoring articles with tenured faculty after the fashion of STEM research publications. Experience in such projects is a great boon on the job market, as more and more departments seek fluency in this field.

All of the above suggestions are aimed at expanding on what medieval and early modern literary studies already do well. There could be more, and I have not even addressed the need for the concept of job placement to be modernized and expanded beyond traditional (and ever-dwindling) academic options. The language and mindset of university research centers—where dollars flow and institutional success stories are shaped and told—might seem antithetical to the humanities, but the disciplines we care about must grit their teeth, smile, and embrace them, at least a little. At stake is the future of those disciplines as viable parts of a university's research mission, not to mention the viability of its students as candidates in a brutally competitive job market.

12/

HISTORY AND COMMITMENT

Guy Halsall

🖙 ITEM: RANKEAN HISTORY IS DEAD

No one will pretend it is possible to tell history as it really was.

But no one has seized the implication of that.

Its empirical ghost remains, although simple factual accuracy sets the bar pretty low for a historical project.

Is the cry 'Rankean History is dead: long live Rankean History'?

Or is it time to explore again the pre-Rankean idea of history as philosophy teaching by example?

ITEM: HISTORY IS NOT "RELEVANT"

History does not tell us "how we got here."

History's value lies in:

i. not believing what you're told;
ii. understanding that the world didn't—and doesn't—have to be like this: there are other ways of doing things;
iii. ethical and political stances are implicit in both; to which we must be committed.

History has no monopoly on these; what sets it apart from other arts, humanities and social sciences might uncontroversially be said to be its focus upon concrete situations and completed actions.

And yet it is there that lies the aporia we must explore.

Fuck reality; fuck endings.

ITEM: HISTORICAL NARRATIVE IS A SERIES OF TEMPORAL SPACES DEFINED AFTER THE EVENT, ENFOLDED, CLOSED UP, BY THE PROCESS OF NARRATION, OF COMPLETION, OF CONCRETION

These spaces are the un- or pre-symbolised pre-historicised temporal Real.

History must open up these spaces, not just to look at the causation of the event that marks its closure.

History must open them to a more attentive—yet critical—listening, which is a listening to our writing of the past as well as to the voices of the past.

Such listening avoids subordination to the usual demands of historical narrative.

It escapes the inevitability—the contingent necessity in Žižek's words—of history, where every letter really does arrive at its destination.

In these spaces everything was still to play for, because people frequently didn't know what they were playing for—they were usually doing something else.

History is what happens while you're making other plans.

These are the spaces of the radically undecided.

Here, the aims of the actors do not necessarily decide the outcome.

Here, things no longer possible remain possible.

These are zones of pure chance and encounter.

☞ITEM: OPENING UP THESE SPACES MAKES US RETHINK HISTORICAL NARRATIVE

This makes the historical narrative inescapably ironic.

It is not the 'what if' history beloved of the Right, where a different throw of the dice *does* abolish chance.

It understands what happened by exploring what didn't.

We furnish a better guide to ethical and politically committed action in the present by restoring to the past its once possible impossibilities.

13/

ON NEVER LETTING GO

Cary Howie

1.

There are a lot of things to be said for letting go. Our attachments can limit us in bad ways as well as good ones; more than once, when saying goodbye to a particular place or person whose future just cannot be mine any longer, I have thought of Alison Krauss affirming, with her usual bittersweetness, "And I'm no longer bound / I can let go now."[1] It is often difficult to cop to the things that bind us; difficult to assess what kind of binding makes us live more intensely and what kind of binding, in contrast, merely constrains us, keeps us from that fuller

---

[1] "I Can Let Go Now," written by Michael McDonald, appears on Alison Krauss and Union Station's album *So Long So Wrong* (Rounder, 1997).

life. Letting go makes room for something, and the whole point is that it's a gamble: you don't know what you're making room for. That determinacy is, among other things, what you're giving up. Similarly, in a different idiom, the classic definition of melancholia is built around a refusal to let go: a refusal to acknowledge what is gone as gone. But in the background of every question about letting go, another question lurks: how do we know that something is gone? And how, by the same token, do we come to terms with the very real presences that continue to surround and define us? That is to say, if melancholia misses its mark because it will not surrender what it aims at, even when what it aims at is gone, there is a kind of complementary malaise that is too cavalier about its terms of surrender, that wants to aim at nothing at all, that wants to give it all up, even those things without which life is, strictly speaking, unimaginable. In these pages I'd like to ask this question, among others: is there a way to honor the risk, the gamble, implicit in our gestures of relinquishment while also affirming the ties that continue to bind us—for the best—to the world? Or, to put it slightly differently, can we let go of certain things—certain professional outcomes, erotic futures, grudges, habits—while holding on to others, without this diminishing our relinquishment?

We can, obviously, and we do. For example, I decide to abandon an old ambition—not, however, as blithely as I tend to think at the time of the decision—while nonetheless embracing another. In fact, it is often my tenacious embrace of this latter ambition (say, the ambition to become better at letting go of things) that allows my relinquishment of the first ambition to happen at all. There are things we have to hold on to, as well as ways of holding on, in order to be able to give anything up. You could, of course, approach the question differently: you could say that the real problem is with words like "aim" and "hold," words that seek to fasten too surely on their objects, words that don't give these objects room, that don't let these objects be. But I am increasingly inclined, these days, to say that there's nothing particularly wrong with aiming and holding. Think, for instance, of those signs you may have seen in the bathroom of a relative's house or a country restaurant: *We Aim To Please; You Aim Too, Please!*

My aim, then, is to appreciate the inherent complication of holding on. We only ever hold on to something by letting go of something else, or even, perhaps, by letting go of this same thing; conversely, our relinquishments are tenacious: they have fingerprints all over them. This isn't so much something to work on as the way things are. In the sixth-century *Mystical Theology* attributed to Dionysius the Areopagite, the whole point of praising God, the whole point of any language extended toward the divine, is that it can only ever really aim. God—as God—falls right out of language, even as this is no excuse to give up on language but, rather, an impetus to say both more and less, to affirm and deny and affirm again, on and on, until your finite tongue stops stammering.[2] Dionysius provides, in this brief treatise, a model of holding on while letting go:

> I pray we could come to this darkness so far above light! If only we lacked sight and knowledge so as to see, so as to know, unseeing and unknowing, that which lies beyond all vision and knowledge. For this would be really to see and to know: to praise the Transcendent One in a transcending way, namely through the denial of all beings. We would be like sculptors who set out to carve a statue. They remove every obstacle to the pure view of the hidden image, and simply by this act of clearing aside they show up the beauty which is hidden.[3]

---

[2] It's more common, these days, to find this acknowledgment that the tongue must do everything it can, even as it falls short of its object, in the rhetoric of erotic experience: witness R. Kelly's "Genius," the first track to be released from the apophatically promising 2013 album *Black Panties*, in which "la-la-la-la-la" marks the limits of language.

[3] Pseudo-Dionysius, *The Complete Works*, trans. Colm Luibheid

Here Dionysius sets aside his nearly unrelenting focus on language for another means of representation and presentation, namely, sculpture. To sculpt a statue out of a given material, according to this passage, requires treating that material as at once the hiding-place of an image and an obstacle to that hidden image's manifestation. In other words, it requires being of two minds—or, better, of two hands—about the material out of which the image will emerge. The stuff you're working with—stone, wood, soap—isn't disposable; it has a certain intractability: if you carved too far or too much, you'd end up with no sculpture at all. The "beauty which is hidden" would stay that way; or, rather, it would become manifest in the beauty of a pile of wood chips and soap curls, a different beauty from that of the sculpted image. If you are more likely to mow than sculpt, think of this as the equivalent of the scalped lawn: in the overzealous clearing aside, what becomes visible is not nothing—it is, for example, dirt and rock and the bees' nest by the neighbors' hydrangeas—but it is not lawn, at least not until the grass comes back.

The text's word for the double movement by which matter is at once negated and intensified is *aphairesis*, "clearing aside," but we could as easily call it letting go while holding on, or holding on while letting go, the relinquishment of something—something as solid as stone—so that it may become differently visible, differently tangible. And how is this relinquishment accomplished? By touching that material stuff—that stone, that body—with particular care, particular incisiveness, cutting into it so that new surfaces—surfaces it has always possessed—become apparent. (To return to scalping: have you had the pleasure of touching recently shaved skin? Of having yours—accidentally or studiously—touched? Have you felt the thrill of the pierced place where, against every expectation, an absence feels paradoxically present, full of some sentience that cannot be strictly new—nothing was added to your body when that hollow was carved out—but must

---

(Mahwah, NJ: Paulist Press, 1987), 138.

have been latent all this time, never not *pierceable*, like water within the struck stone?) This is one way of saying that what constitutes the "hidden image" for Dionysius is not something *other than* the very material stuff within which the image waits to be disclosed; it is not some other—and it is certainly not some more ethereal or abstract—thing. The image which lies within the stone, which shows itself only when some of its surrounding stuff is carved away or cleared aside, cannot be apprehended without—even as it remains irreducible to—the stone.

2.

Hold on. To praise the "Transcendent One in a transcending way" is to climb, through language, toward what exceeds language, even as it remains (transcendently, Dionysius would stress) the ground and source and basic stuff of language. But what about those of us for whom the question of a "Transcendent One" is, at best, a question and, at worst, a metaphysical fantasy? What if the transcending way is all we've got—and, even then, less likely to be transcending than reiterating, tracing one of innumerable paths through a substance it never quite gets beyond? This would amount to saying that there is no hidden image lurking within the statue; that what we find is what we make: the only certainty is in the work, terminal (we all end, sooner or later, at least apparently) and (in the meantime) interminable. I'm not sure that this makes a difference, to be honest, within the uncompromising terms of the Dionysian dialectic: on the one hand, the Transcendent One is so utterly in excess of even our most rigorous rhetoric, our most surgical sculpture, that it remains ultimately hidden (and one could well imagine objections, on the part of a fleshier theology, to just this hiddenness); on the other hand, the ordinary work of our hands never ceases to let and to latch, to hold and to put on hold, whether or not this movement participates in a larger cosmic dialectic of procession and return.

To bring this down to earth: I am carving away at the stuff of my life and watching for what emerges; and suddenly something I thought intrinsic to the work—for example, a particular professional identity and source of income—ends up in the shavings. The work becomes distinct, for me, from the job—and this, in an age as strictly professionalized as our own, is huge—only as I take leave of the job, only as I realize that it has perhaps already taken leave of me. The transcending way is a reciprocal leave-taking (although it is not always a symmetrical one: you can leave it before it leaves you, or vice-versa). Maybe this is only an elaborate way of stating the ambivalences that attend any work, the ease with which any work can be confused with the scripts into which it's written (professional scripts, paradigmatically, but also those of social class, taste, geography, kinship), but it is, I find, especially important to insist on the simultaneous necessity and goodness of carving away at the stuff of our lives, even if this means (for example) that the work relinquishes the job, relinquishes the prestige and security that may have attended the job, just as language relinquishes its object in the process of straining toward some more fundamental, more propulsive object which would, finally, be no object at all.

For, even as I write from a position of relatively great professional security, this is one of the things that I cannot let go of: that this work of my hands—these words you've taken the time to read—remains distinct from, even as it remains indebted to, what I claim (in one of the less felicitous idioms of our language) to do for a living. When things are going well—when my colleagues at home or at large honor what I do—it's easy to forget this distinction. But when the transcending way becomes a rocky road, when there emerges some incommensurability between my work and my job, then the distinction becomes as clear as the light that, on this windy September afternoon, is shining on the undersides of leaves, their more secret places. This emergence may happen because of something I've done—some stand I've taken, some refusal to abide by the profession's written or unwritten rules—or something I've left undone; or it may happen without cause, without why. If I am lucky, or if I am attentive, someone may show me some kindness in the process; amid the myriad unkindnesses of the world, in some of which I am inevitably complicit, there may emerge some gaze, some touch, that holds on to me as it honors my leave-taking, as it sees me off into that world which is my own, my only, work.[4]

3.

"The Silent Angel," a prose poem by James Wright, contains another hidden image, a kindly one, equally inseparable from the stuff out of which it emerges. The speaker is sitting on a bus at the gate of Verona, Italy, where a man "standing in one of the pink marble arches of the great Roman arena" smiles at him. This man holds the speaker's gaze—"his knowing eyes never leaving me"—for the entire time the bus is stopped at the gate, and even as it pulls away; and the poem ends with the angel waving goodbye "as kindly as he could" while holding "what seemed to be a baton":

> ... and it hung suspended for a long instant in the vast petals of rose shadows cast down by the marble walls. Even after he had vanished back into the archway, I could still see his hand.[5]

Wright's angel, as he emerges from and retreats into the marble arches of Verona, seems as good an analogue as any for the sculptural clearing that Dionysius has described. Not just because this is marble, sculptable stone— yet notice how the hand does not manipulate the marble

---

[4] In Mary Oliver's poem "Messenger," her speaker affirms, "My work is loving the world." It is possible to love the world through my professional activities, but when those activities keep me from loving the world, it is time to let them go. See Mary Oliver, *Thirst* (Boston: Beacon, 2006), 1.

[5] James Wright, "The Silent Angel," *To a Blossoming Pear Tree* (New York: Farrar, Straus and Giroux, 1977), 49.

but rather becomes visible amidst its "rose shadows"—but also, and more crucially, because the angel in the arches is neither dispensable nor sufficient, neither something the speaker can hold on to (for any longer than the scheduled bus stop) nor something he can entirely let go of. The hand, which persists in the speaker's field of vision even after the rest of the angel has "vanished," is a token of the persistence of the visible angelic body, and of the speaker's desire to see, even as the vision itself is destined to be temporary, as well as rose-colored. The speaker is on a bus, after all, and that bus is leaving the marble arena. The speaker is being transported in a way that is, strictly speaking, independent of the angel's epiphany, and he's being carried not toward the source of this epiphany but away from it. The hand only becomes visible in its retreat.

What is cleared away, among other things, in this poem is all of the distraction and phenomenological noise that can keep one body from holding another, even holding another in its field of vision, for even the briefest of moments; what is cleared away is everything but the arena, and the bus, and the smile, and the baton, and the hand. Through this clearing—this clearing which just *is* poetic language, a denial not of materiality per se but of certain instances of matter so that others might shine more brightly, a privileging of particular material persons, and phonemes, and things, so that the material itself might not be forgotten—through this rose-petal clearing an image comes to view. The speaker has not attained that image (which is itself constantly being displaced: smile, hand, baton) much less to the source of that image; but the image has lingered long enough to hint *that* there is a source; that something beckons from the shadows; or—if this sounds too much like a Transcendent One— that there is, at least, a beckoning. Something is waving to you even as you take your leave. Someone is seeing you off. Hold on to that. Better yet, allow it to hold you as it lets you go.

4.

In a poem called "Insertion of Meadow with Flowers," Mary Szybist writes: "Out of nothing does not mean // into nothing."[6] If it is important to recognize—and not just to recognize but to say, again and again—the nothing out of which all things come, in such a way that "nothing" is not heard as the opposite of "something," in such a way that nothing is not ontologically comprehensible (not even as negation), how much more important is it to say the things into which nothing comes, as well as the break across which their advent happens, across which an advent is still happening? Even as we take leave, even as we let go, we don't spiral into the void. Something comes into and near and as our bodies, our souls, our work. In her poem, God comes into a meadow as flowers, of which Szybist writes: "and they are infused / with what they did not / reach for." Not only is it the case that God, for Dionysius, remains beyond every reach while inviting us to keep reaching; here it may not ultimately matter whether we reach at all. Szybist's poem cautions us not to take the Dionysian dialectic too seriously—not to treat it as exhaustive—but, above all, to pay attention—I swear that the goldenrod was not there yesterday—when suddenly something blooms. You are already being infused with something you did not ask for, something greater (and less) than the sum of what you thought your life added up to. You, too, are an image carved from something; you are a friendly hand emerging from a stone shadow. To ape a famous lyric: once you have found it, never let it go. Once you have found it—once you have seen it waving from the shadows, once it has blossomed beneath and within the weight of your body—it will never let you go.[7]

---

[6] Mary Szybist, "Insertion of Meadow with Flowers," *Incarnadine* (Minneapolis: Graywolf, 2013), 61.
[7] These are the words of Richard Rodgers and Oscar Hammerstein II's "Some Enchanted Evening," from their 1949 musical *South Pacific*.

14/

THE GOTHIC FLY

Shayne Aaron Legassie

Gore Verbinski's 2002 film *The Ring* is a remake of the popular Japanese horror movie *Ringu* (1998), directed by Hideo Nakata. Both films tell the story of a cursed videotape whose viewers die gruesome deaths seven days after they watch it. At the level of both plot and visual style, Verbinski's departures from *Ringu* are deeply indebted to the conventions of the gothic novel, especially as they were mediated by European and American cinema. This gothic aesthetic "translates" *Ringu* into a more familiar Hollywood idiom for the benefit of North American viewers. Many of *The Ring's* gothic innovations have long pedigrees, some of which stretch back to premodern painting and thought.

Take, for example, a scene from *The Ring* that has no precedent in *Ringu*. The film's protagonist Rachel (played by Naomi Watts) tries to uncover the secrets of the sinister video in the A/V lab of the newspaper where she works [Figs. 1, 2 and 3]. In the course of examining the recording's bizarre procession of images, Rachel makes an alarming discovery. A fly that appears to be superimposed over a forlorn seascape pulsates with life even after she pauses the tape. The fly is in—but not *of*—the video recording. Mesmerized, Rachel reaches out to the screen and manages to pull the insect out of the television.

Fig. 1: Something strange afoot, *The Ring*

Fig. 2: Crossing worlds, *The Ring*

Fig. 3: Capture as Knowledge

The Ring's fly is part of a long aesthetic and intellectual history that equates knowledge of the cosmos with knowledge of the fly, and knowledge of the fly with its realistic capture by the visual arts. Its most obvious ancestor is the impudent fellow who seems to scurry across the bottom of the frame (also an optical illusion) of Petrus Christus' *Portrait of a Carthusian* (1446), now in the Metropolitan Museum of Art in New York City [Fig. 4].

The boundary-defying fly is frequently found at the center of artistic and epistemological myths of origin, including the legendary beginning of cinematic special effects. Spanish cinematographer Segundo de Chomón—a pioneer of stop-motion photography—claimed that he stumbled upon the technique when a fly stumbled *into* his camera's apparatus. When Chomón projected the invaded film, the insect seemed to move across the screen as if it were alive.[1] We encounter the fly at the supposed beginnings of modern painting, as well. In a legend popularized by Vasari, Giotto is said to have deceived his master Cimabue by painting a fly on the older artist's canvas. When Cimabue tried to brush it away, the pupil's superi-

---

[1] José María Candel, *Historia del dibujo animado español* (Murcia: Ed. Regional, 1993), 20.

ority was confirmed.[2] For Vasari, Giotto's triumph heralds a new era, a movement toward the unparalleled realism of mathematical perspective. The belief that medieval painting was archaic laid the groundwork for the eighteenth-century invention of the ambivalent, and always anachronistic, term "Gothic," used to describe both late medieval artistic technique and the spirit of the Age.

Fig. 4: Petrus Christus, *Portrait of a Carthusian,* oil on wood. With permission of the Metropolitan Museum of Art, New York.

Paradoxically, Giotto's supposedly epoch-shifting "renaissance" fly actually has its origins in the "Gothic" era manuscript painting. The *Visconti Hours*' (Florence:

---

[2] Andrew Ladis, *Victims and Villains in Vasari's* Lives (Chapel Hill, NC: UNC Press, 2008), 10–11.

BNF Ms. BR 259, fol. 19) depiction of the creation of the Earth, painted around 1390, does not *represent* the fly to the same scale that it does other flora and fauna; instead, it *renders* it as though it has landed on the page. The flies arrayed around the "in principio" of *Genesis* reference a commentary tradition in which the fly was created belatedly, after Adam and Eve's exile from Eden. This argument rested on the commonly held belief that the fly generated spontaneously from corrupt matter, and therefore inhabited a biological and eschatological temporality that overlapped with human history, but marched to a different tempo. It is not surprising, then, to find the trompe l'oeil fly looking from a distance onto the imagined end of times, as well—as one does beneath the famous painting of the Apocalypse in the *Très Riches Heures* (Chantilly: MC ms. 65, fol. 17r). Wherever there is an uncanny doubling of beginnings or an ending that is at the same time a new beginning, there you will find the haunt of the gothic fly.

Fig. 5: Ambivalent Angels, *Grizzly Man*

In its formal and thematic treatment of the fly, cinema is shaped by ideas and pictorial conventions—and ideas embedded within pictorial conventions—that one might be tempted to view as strictly "medieval." Yet, they resound on into the age of cinema, making a mockery of tidy epochal distinctions. The unrealistic pitch and timbre with which the fly is almost always rendered in sound cinema evokes the possibility that it hails from a different reality. The cinematic fly often seems like a divine herald of new beginnings or the harbinger of death. This is true not just of horror film, but even of documentary. Who has seen the final sequence of Werner Herzog's *Grizzly Man* (2005) and *not* experienced the sensation that the flies that buzz about the camera and land on its lens are birds of bad omen or messengers from beyond our sensual world [Fig. 5]?

The moral of this minifesto: Film criticism should be considered part of what we do *as medievalists*, and not something that we do *in addition to* Medieval Studies.

15/

FUCK POSTCOLONIALISM

Erin Maglaque

Since the late 1990s, a group of medieval literary scholars and historians have drawn upon postcolonial theory, a discipline which itself emerged, in its most coherent and resilient form, from the Subaltern Studies group fifteen years before.[1] Medievalists' work with postcolonial theory can be roughly divided into two kinds of engagement: first is the group of scholars interested in applying postcolonial theories to their medieval sources, and who are, in the tradition of Said's *Orientalism*, interested in the representative work of the racial or ethnic other in the medieval text.[2] A second and perhaps more disparate

---

[1] Postcolonial theory was initially introduced to medieval studies in Kathleen Biddick's *The Shock of Medievalism* (London: Duke University Press, 1998).
[2] See the essays collected in Jeffrey Jerome Cohen, ed., *The Post-*

group is interested in the disciplinary and political implications of medievalism and postcolonialism, their intertwined intellectual histories, and especially the ways in which studying the interrelation between postcolonial and medieval historiographies can lead to a reconsideration of periodization and temporalities.[3]

With the publication in 2013 of Vivek Chibber's *Postcolonial Theory and the Specter of Capital*, though, it is time for a serious reconsideration of the role and function of postcolonial theory within medieval studies.[4] Published by Verso Press, this book has been intensely debated in the world of Marxist political blogging, although its presence has perhaps not yet been felt in more mainstream academic circles.[5] Chibber writes a persuasive, compelling dismantling of the Subaltern Studies group that demonstrates that their central historical and theoretical premises are flawed. In brief, Chibber argues that the Subalternists' model of understanding the east as fundamentally different from the west, and the subsequent need for a distinct, indigenous theory to describe these differences, are based on a misunderstanding of both western and eastern history. Chibber describes the spread of capitalism in India and shows that it was, in specific ways 'central to economic reproduction,' highly similar to the adoption of capitalism in Europe.[6] The process of becoming modern—for Chibber, a process which was one and

---

colonial Middle Ages (Basingstoke, UK: Macmillan, 2000).

[3] See Patricia Clare Ingham and Michelle R. Warren, eds., *Postcolonial Moves: Medieval Through Modern* (New York: Palgrave Macmillan, 2003); and Kathleen Davis and Nadia Altschul, *Medievalisms in the Postcolonial World: The Idea of the 'Middle Ages' Outside Europe* (Baltimore: Johns Hopkins University Press, 2009).

[4] Chibber, Vivek. *Postcolonial Theory and the Specter of Capital* (London: Verso, 2013).

[5] See, for instance, an interview with Chibber published in Jacobin Magazine, available online at: http://jacobinmag.com/2013/04/how-does-the-subaltern-speak/, and the debate between Chris Tayloy and Paul M. Heideman archived on the Verso blog, available at: http://www.versobooks.com/authors/1734-vivek-chibber.

[6] Chibber, *Postcolonial Theory and the Specter of Capital*, 248.

the same as that of the adoption of capitalism—was designed to be described by Marxism; if this process happened in the same way across the globe, then Marxism can very well describe the historical sociology of these effects. Not only is there no need for postcolonial theory, then, but postcolonial theory actually works negatively to minimize the impact of global capitalism, and to effectively orientalize the Indian peasant by characterizing him as antithetical to the individualism, rationality, objectivity, and familiarity of western European history.

If for Chibber, the history of the global spread of capitalism is the history of colonialism, we might wonder where exactly this leaves medievalists. We could argue that it is precisely the temporal colonization of the Middle Ages for various disciplinary and political ends that gives us an opportunity to problematize Chibber's argument. After all, in taking the English and French Revolutions as central moments in his inquiry—moments that were of course central to Marx, too—Chibber posits an imagined medieval feudal origin, parallel to the kind of medieval literary origins that Kathleen Biddick has so persuasively argued for in Said's work.[7] The alternative chronologies and temporalities described by the Subalternists for the global south and by the Annalistes for agrarian Europe, though, simply do not hold up under Chibber's analysis: the Indian and European peasant was not excluded from modernity, but their political agencies and resistances were rather formed in the face of capital's universalizing drive. Bruce Holsinger's illuminating article on the relationship between the Annalistes and Subalternists becomes even more important in this context, for as Holsinger demonstrates, the postcolonial theorization of a Subaltern 'politics of time' was influenced by their reading of medievalist Annaliste agrarian histories.[8] The Annalistes saw the European peasantry as having existed on

---

[7] Kathleen Biddick, "Coming Out of Exile: Dante on the Orient Express," in Cohen, ed., *The Postcolonial Middle Ages*, 35–52.
[8] Bruce Holsinger, "Medieval Studies, Postcolonial Studies, and the Genealogies of Critique," *Speculum* 77.4 (2002): 1195–1227.

a different temporal scale than the urban bourgeois—a slower, longer, premodern scale—which excluded them from conventional Marxist narratives of modernity. Chibber's central point that to be excluded from capitalist modernity is not to exist within an alternate temporality, but rather to have one's political agency and social relationships defined and deeply influenced by capitalism, is thus of considerable importance both for postcolonial theorists and medievalists alike.

Chibber argues that postcolonial theory should not have a future at all, as it simultaneously 'obscures the very forces that drive the political dynamics' in the global south and 'promot[es] conceptions of it that are systematically misleading.'[9] For Chibber, Marxism is not only adequate to describing the political dynamics of modern India, but actually designed specifically to explain it; Marxism is the only theoretical toolkit we need to explain the 'unequal and uneven forces of cultural representation involved in the contest for political and social authority.'[10] Ignoring the importance of the universalization of capital whilst still waving the postcolonialist banner for leftist academia is thus, as Slavov Žižek proclaims pugnaciously on the cover of Chibber's book, to contribute to the 'stale aroma of the pseudo-radical academic establishment.' If the parallels between the ways in which India and the Middle Ages have been treated as objects of historical inquiry can stand up, and I believe that they do, then we need to take seriously Chibber's challenge to postcolonial theory, as well as his defense of Marxism.

What do the misrepresentations of the Subalternists mean for medieval studies? I would suggest that from the Subalternist theorization of east and west as irreconcilably historically different—founded, as Chibber has shown, on shaky historical analysis—medievalists have shaped their research around questions of temporal difference, circling around the 'traumas' of periodization, alterity,

---

[9] Chibber, *Postcolonial Theory and the Specter of Capital*, 293.
[10] Cohen quoting Homi Bhabha, "Midcolonial," in Cohen, ed., *The Postcolonial Middle Ages*, 3.

and disciplinary ghettoization. These indeed may be important questions to ask, but to attempt to answer them by leaning on a theoretical (Subalternist, postcolonial) framework which has been historically undermined is to be uncritical and, perhaps more destructively, to work actively to obscure. In using postcolonial theory to lend institutional capital to medieval studies, and to appear as intellectually radical—and therefore fashionable—to our departments, universities, and peers, we obscure a truly radical political agenda; using postcolonial theory allows us to feel radical without being radical, and so promotes political complacency. It has allowed us to retreat further and further into the often alienating, complicated language of Subalternist theory, and the echo chamber of the literature departments within our universities. At a time when the left is under serious attack, it is more important than ever that we shed the institutional coziness of 'pseudo-radical' postcolonial theory, for a mode of historical inquiry that is alive to the radical possibilities of similarity and universality, rather than difference.

16/

WE ARE THE MATERIAL COLLECTIVE

Material Collective

We are the Material Collective, a group of medievalists interrogating visual materials. We seek to:

> cooperate
> encourage
> share
> promote transparency
> touch
> desire
> destabilize
> amuse
> blunder

As a collaborative of students of visual culture, Material Collective seeks to foster a safe space for alternative ways of thinking about objects.

We strive for transparency in our practice, and we encourage the same in our institutional surroundings.

Our project touches upon both form and content, as we pursue a lyrical and experimental style of writing along with a more humane, collaborative, and supportive process of scholarship.

We encourage spontaneity in writing art history, including an acknowledgement of our subject positions;

therefore we embrace the incorporation of personal narrative and reflection in our historical interpretations.

Our specific interests vary, but we are all committed to prioritizing the materiality of things, the relationships between those things and the human beings who experience them, and the intimacy of past and present moments in time.

As we celebrate, dwell in, and embrace the basic materiality of our objects, we work to find ways to foreground the material of the objects themselves into larger historical analysis.

Central to this effort is a desire to support each other as we attempt to create experimental approaches, and to embrace both the successes and potential failures of our ventures into new ways of thinking.

We are also working to increase the legitimacy of these approaches in the academic world, primarily by *practicing* them, *loudly and often.*

We are as much a support group as a scholarly group. We share the joys and sorrows of career, life and our academic work.

For us, this is not a mere exercise—we stand by our manifesto.

we value:

experimental processes
risk-taking
transparency, revelation
a blank space
joy in faltering, together

**so say we all
so say we all**

The manifesto was co-composed by the following Material Collective members:

*Marian Bleeke
Jennifer Borland
Rachel Dressler
Martha Easton
Martin K. Foys
Anne F. Harris
Asa Simon Mittman
Karen Overbey
Angela Bennett Segler
Ben C. Tilghman
Nancy M. Thompson
Maggie M. Williams*

17/

MEDIEVALISM/SURREALISM

Thomas Mical

1.

This is a question concerning architecture. An immersion into the imaginary worlds, specifically the fusion of an imaginary world into the everyday real, was the great project of surrealism. The surrealist avant-garde sought to open up a supra-sensory milieu of impossible relations, including monstrous bodies, irrational hybrids, genre mutations, forbidden landscapes and gardens, and a whole range of partial co-located figures and gestures, half real and half other. Surrealism was the promise of a world of alterity and delight, capable of emerging or erupting at the slightest provocation, in the subtlest peripheral glimpse of a disfiguration, and in the recall of the sense and feel of a new space (déjà vu, already sensed). Surrealism is the obverse of modern rationalism, both intersecting but incomplete projects. It is from this call that unrecognized medieval alterity can diversify medieval architectural history beyond the monumental history of differentiated cathedrals (and walled cities).

How can we disregard a monstrous creature, for example, who is an invitation to a world of alterity?

2.

Surrealism is the promise of every form of rationalism, perhaps even the destination of rationalism.[1] Accustomed to rationalism today, the surreal seems eccentric, a fringe activity. But what if we postulate that in many medieval practices, often it was rationalism that was the exception. The negotiated everyday reality of religion, superstition, folklore, experience, wisdom, emotion, erring, heresy, and all forms of categorical contingency must have made people think. And thinking is really what was at stake in surrealism. Breton famously defined surrealism as "Psychic automatism in its pure state, by which one proposes to express—verbally, by means of the written word, or in any other manner—the actual functioning of thought."[2] Salvador Dalí takes this to an extreme, when he states, "I believe the moment is at hand when, by a process of thought which is active and paranoiac in character, it will be possible ... to systematize confusion and to contribute to the total discredit of the world of reality."[3] Fantasy, delusion, and disfiguration become the end-game of rea-

---

[1] Koolhaas' analysis of the Paranoiac-Critical method of Salvador Dalí is found in Rem Koolhaas, *Delirious New York* (New York: Monacelli Press, 1994); see also the explanation by Jamer Hunt, "Paranoid, Critical, Methodical, Dalí, Koolhass, and ... ," in George E. Marcus, *Paranoia within Reason: A Casebook on Conspiracy as Explanation* (Chicago: University of Chicago Press, 1999), 21–30.
[2] Andre Breton, *Manifestoes of Surrealism* (1924; repr. Ann Arbor: University of Michigan Press, 1972), 25.
[3] Salvador Dalí, *Oui: The Paranoid-Critical Revolution: Writings 1927-1933* (Boston: Exact Change, 1998), 115.

son. How can we come to know these irrational or nonsensical aspects and aspirations, were they to occur in the medieval mind? Can Aquinas (or Foucault) tell me how to think and build surreally, or medievally? Obviously the surrealist project is to replace banal reality with a superior form of reality, a surreality, often initiated from a subjectivity operating at micro-scale.

Architecture needs more surrealism, just as it needs more medievalism.

3.

Select medieval sources in Surrealism can be located in the thoughts of Bataille, in his posthumous *Unfinished System of Non-Knowledge*; or in Erin Felicia Labbie's *Lacan's Medievalism*; or even a stretch to Umberto Eco's *On Ugliness*. The term "Medieval Surrealism" actually sources from an early essay on the poetic-visionary architect John Hejduk, nominated to circumscribe his speculative worldview, a projection of imaginary and arcane architectural speculations.[4] This subjective investigation required the difficulty of assembling allegories mated with allegories, enigmas emerging from enigmas, into a cascade of fallen "angels" of thought that combine and condense the figures of thought with the thought itself. The medieval qualities were the rough tectonics and the subversion of rational functionalism through transcendent narrative = powerful projections. The reciprocal relation, of the presence of surrealism within medievalism, seems self-evident. Here, Bosch and Breughel can dominate the (irrational) marvelous landscape. Indeed, the disorientation of many medieval thought patterns may read initially as surreal, and for this reason the surreal seems at home in much medievalist thought and practice, not as a totalizing discourse, but as an invitation to an opening. The medieval corpus texts and images are but incomplete evidence

---

[4] David A. Greenspan, "Medieval Surrealism," *Inland Architect* 2 (1981): 10–29.

of the lure of other worlds of fascination, waiting (like condensation) to appear on the surfaces of this world. Fevers, obsessions, possession, madness, and the emergence of a subsequent Romanticist unconscious—all are exposed as a system by Foucault—even the hysterical absurd Chinese encyclopaedia. [5] There are a great many proto-surrealist operations in surviving medieval works, waiting to be exposed and dried and examined and re-animated. Indeed, the dividing line or distinction between the surreal and non-surreal in medieval works might be less useful than the sympathetic resonances and fertile possibilities of the respective contamination and fusion of the real and imaginary, as surrealism presupposes.

As surrealist thought is projected backwards, as medieval thoughts are projected forward, the irrational will condense clearly.

4.

This speculative medievalist-surrealist approach (under development) is not intended as an anachronistic or reactionary counter-medievalism, but is intended to plea for the force of the imagination as movement as the ultimate conceptual transformer and spatial shape-shifter. Let us reframe medieval surrealism as a material practice, dependent on unconventional thought systems, a thinking though making. Much of medieval aesthetics exceeds the rational, or the spiritual, and often exists in tension with the limits of the sensual. These are the transitive markers of the movements of thought, artifacts and images primarily. Close attention to the bodily knowledge of medieval cobblers, tinkers, and especially masons reveal advanced design intelligences excluded from texts, and their works are thought experiments within complex systems of knowledge. But the bestiary of medieval thought fuses this with non-knowledge. From this, the bricoleur, the

---

[5] Michel Foucault, *The Order of Things: An Archaeology of the Human Sciences* (London: Routledge, 2002), xvi.

heretic, the alchemist can be seen as exceptions, working and re-working what cannot fit. The analogues of thought in the process of making evident in medieval architecture provide a body of evidence that itself is cobbled together, like an annotated medieval treatise, from an irregular variety of sources and works, selectively pursued to resemble the generative original vision or impulse that is exquisite, desirable, and impossible, all at the same time. Surrealist creation is a modern problem, masking a medieval problem.

We make what we need as a rationalization of what we desire.

5.

The medieval world begins one space at a time. There is more than one medieval world, and the architectural tableaux (created by guild or informal construction) exist within a fabric of possible worlds, and therefore possible meanings. We assume none of these are fixed or singular, even in orthodoxy, even when Panofsky, in *Gothic Architecture and Scholasticism*, determines the musical basis of the cathedral-lattices. In Umberto Eco's *Postscript to Name of the Rose*, he identifies three forms of labyrinth to explain explanation: classical, baroque, rhizomatic. Indeed, the architect has historically been obsessed with labyrinths, from Daedalus to *Inception*, as the site of folding multiple worlds together.[6] Intersection, interpenetration, transmutation are developed, not given, between medieval worlds—the mix of classes and societies is a commerce and exchange of realties, of the inevitable dissonance of rival realities, which is formative and legible in the aesthetics and ruins of medieval building or in any presentation of a medieval world (alternative evidence of an alternative world). The monstrous in the fabric of everyday

---

[6] One example of the new knowledge of intersecting world is my book project, T. Mical, *Mies and Negative Theology* (in progress).

life is nothing new, indeed the function of monster theory is to de-familiarize the familiar, creating errant, deformed, and uncanny doubles, often of our own unmaking (and undoing). Breughel's mutations (think "Foucault meets David Lynch") are avant-garde examples of the singular monster as a harbinger of another world, one lurking under the surface or around the corner of our perceptions. World-building and system-building are the primary making-thinking couple, arising from a medieval fertility of imagination. The role of the eccentric and the grotesque are formative principles and passions—imaginary cartographies and irrational systems, taxonomies, bestiaries populate the artistic and creative imagination. Compare Ginzburg's *The Cheese and the Worms* with any subsequent architectural treatise. We need more Focillon and Frankl when they question or dare to indulge in speculation on the eccentric and abnormal at the limits of medieval architecture.

The eccentric is always a possible new topography, the grotesque is always a genesis of a possible world.

6.

The medieval imagination is the missing FORCE behind the range of medieval building projects, and related creative guild practices. Medieval Architectural Intelligence stretches across habit to cunning into the impossible imagination, but it must also include those fevers, obsessions, possession, madness, and the proto-unconscious. And for this reason, surrealism, as a theoretical artistic practice, offers a way into this system of knowledge and non-knowledge. The power of the medieval imagination is a force. It could carve though huge blocks of inherited knowledge and pre-formatted discourses (aesthetics, angelic theology, ethics) while rising up imaginary structures where the mason would only live to se a few meters progress in one lifetime. The Medieval Architectural Intelligence, and not the conventional sequence of cathedrals, would be a true object of analysis for medieval research tasty to architects today, one where humanist eccentricities, desires, conceits, errors, adventures, and all forms of arabesques of distraction and irrationality would place in the discourse. We could even imagine mock-scientific ('paraphysical') force diagrams of the medieval imagination, so as to annotate our study of worlds created and broken through this force—a type of research more like a conceptual ballistics test.

> God is the point of tangency between zero and infinity.
> Alfred Jarry[7]

The term "Medieval Surrealism" comes from an early essay on the poetic-visionary architect John Hejduk and it is perhaps John Hejduk who is also the source of this line of inquiry. This synthetic and synthesizing construct-become-method is cobbled together, like an annotated medieval treatise, from an irregular variety of sources and works, selectively pursued to resemble the generative original vision or impulse. It is meant to be majestic instead of rigorous, based on parallelisms and minimally perceptible equivalencies, but also with the investigation of a fascination that sometimes requires the difficulty of assembling allegories mated with allegories, enigmas emerging from enigmas, into a cascade of fallen "angels" of thought that combine and condense the figures of thought with the thought itself, here a consideration of a new biomorphic recombinant theory of the imagination drawn form medieval and surrealist sources, as well as obscure sources like Rene Thom's catastrophe theory, Foucault's Chinese encyclopedia, and always the menace of Alfred Jarry's own 'pataphyscis—the science of exceptions—where God is the tangential point between zero and infinity."

There are a great many medieval sources and operations in surrealism (itself an exquisite and marvellous form of modernism), as there are a great many proto-

---

[7] Alfred Jarry, *Exploits and Opinions of Dr. Faustroll, Pataphysician* (1911; repr. Boston: Exact Change, 1996), 91.

surrealist operations in surviving medieval works. Indeed, the dividing line or distinction is less useful than the sympathies, resonances, and fertile possibilities of their respective contamination and fusion. The speculative methodology of "medieval surrealism" is situated within our own time (here taken to be a hybrid-monstrous late modernism). The overwhelming persistence of our hyper-transparency and hyper-immediacy of images can overwhelm any reading, thinking, or designing process. This speculative medieval surrealist approach is not intended as an anachronistic or reactionary counter-modernity, but is intended to echo the medieval and surrealist tendencies still latent and pulsating in the late modern world today. Aside from the appearance that the late modern condition shares many of the some difficulties and complexities of the high Middle Ages, our attention should remain focused upon a singular topic—"the imaginary." It is for this question, of *the potentiality of the medieval surrealist imaginary to active the emergence of the new*, that a neo-medieval vision must be crafted—as a plea for the force of the imagination as movement as the ultimate transformer and shape-shifter, whether these be monsters or angels.

18/

DE CATERVIS CETERIS

Chris Piuma

Look, I'm fine, and you're probably fine, and this is all lovely and fine, and I don't really have any complaints, and I don't want to stand here honking and screaming and telling you that you have to do this and you can't do that, because really I'm fine, and you're fine, and this is all lovely and fine, and I have my ways of doing my thing, and you all have your ways of doing your thing, and we have developed and will continue to develop ways of communicating and connecting and intersecting and intercalating and networking and perverting and permuting and exchanging and pollinating and multiplying and shuffling and alphabetizing and taxonimizing and translating and transposing and creatively mishearing and misreading and assembling and reassembling and pleasuring and tantalizing and polishing and abrading and interrogating and sculpting and remodeling and renovating and flipping and overturning and revolutionizing and transcending and eventually nostalgically or elegiacally recalling and reciting and reenacting and recreating and repositioning and reconsidering and reattaching our various things like so many Lego bricks or Tinkertoys or sexual organs, and this is fine, and I'm fine, and you're F-I-N-E fine, and this is all lovely and fine, but, and this is a small but, there's a little thing I'm worried about, or maybe not worried about but maybe bored by, or maybe not bored by but frustrated with, or maybe I'm frustrated and bored and a little worried, even though I'm fine, and this isn't meant to detract from your own fineness, or how lovely and fine all this is, because it really is lovely and fine and you really are fine, but: Could you stop talking about England? Could you stop talking about English literature quite all the time? Or English history? Or English art or whatever? Although really, English literature. And I know that you've tried and I know that twenty years ago, even ten years ago, even five years ago, even last year it was worse, but perhaps you're unaware that you—the collective you, the aggregate you, the blurry you—are still so assured in the self-evident centrality of English. And, in a way, you know, it's fine, English literature is fine, I enjoy it, you enjoy it, it's interesting, there's lots of interesting stuff to talk about about it, we could talk about it all day, you're going to talk about it all day, and you can, that's your thing, and it's fine, and you're fine, and you do a great job talking about it, and it's all lovely and fine, and if medieval English literature were all the literature in the world then really would that be so bad?, it could be worse!, and so why should I be worried or frustrated or bored that your sense of medieval literature is so doggedly focused on English literature, OK there was some blurring between English and French at the time so maybe also French literature, we all love Marie de France, but perhaps not as much as we all love Chaucer, I love Chaucer, you love Chaucer, we all love Chaucer, some of you are Chaucer online, and Chaucer's fine, and I'm fine, and

you're fine, and talking about Chaucer is lovely and fine, and we could talk about him all day, in any number of ways, to talk about whatever else we want to talk about, and so what else do we need? We're practically self-sufficient here: a tale of Chaucer, a loaf of Theory, and thou. And this is a lovely way to spend a day and all this makes perfect sense, especially for those of us who are Americans, because we speak English, and English came from England, and America came from England, right?, and it's really important to remind ourselves, and especially our students, and, when we can, the general public that we have a strong and a natural connection to England by virtue of living in America, no matter what our individual backgrounds are, and so of course if we're studying literature we're going to study English literature, America→English, English→England, thus
   America→England,
     America→England,
       America→England,
         America→England,
           America→England,
             America→England,
               America→England,
                 America→England,
                   America→England,
and we don't need the rest of the world—we don't even need the rest of the UK—because I'm fine, and you're fine, and this is all lovely and fine, and we're all having a great time, and we could do this all day, and surely we're smart enough that we'd notice if there were a problem here, and we can be proud of ourselves, because taking the medieval seriously—hell, taking literature seriously—in this world, in this time, in this country, in this economy, is radical enough. And anyway, who the fuck wants to learn all those languages.

19/

2ND PROGRAM OF THE ORNAMENTALISTS
PREPARED FOR THE ORNAMENTALIST DELEGATION TO THE 47TH INTERNATIONAL CONGRESS ON MEDIEVAL STUDIES, KALAMAZOO, MI

Daniel C. Remein

A.

We, the Ornamentalists, anarcho-eco-pacificist amateurs, advocate an aesthetics of historical cosmicity as the ground of an ethics of medieval studies, an avant-garde poetics, and a revolutionary politics of elaborating a varied cosmos as Public Park. In the face of the current planetary ecological disaster and its goads—the State and Capitalism—a radical reorientation of our interface with the Cosmos is necessary. For medieval studies to begin to adequately respond, it must move aside from the impulse to *thematize* the cultural and the ecological or to *describe* their mutual transversal as thematized by medieval literature. Instead, we must MAKE (as in POETICS). We must elaborate non- and de-instrumentalized ethics and procedures that allow interface with the non-Human Cosmos.[1]

A1.

All decoration is medieval. And so, because certain Ornamentalists feel the affect of interest increased in intensity by the medieval, we accordingly desire that medieval studies contribute to the anarchic occupation of everywhere as Park by a provisionally distinct humanity in complicity with what is outside of that provisional humanity. We would leverage this multiplication of interest as the ground of an intensification of interface with the non-human GROUND from which the human arises in complexity. This leveraging requires a recalibration of the basic function and *posture* of medieval studies in A COMPLETE REJECTION OF THE CONCEPT OF "OBJECT OF STUDY" that would follow from a cosmology of variety to a phenomenology of difference to the pavilion of serious medieval*ism*: an anarchically accessible phenomenological tent that registers as actual in terms of Physics itself. Make shelters with, not knowledge of, the Middle Ages. *We have only* to set aside entirely the symbolic and representational structures and functions of language in favor of the obvious cosmicity of language, determined by its ornamentality.

B.

Cosmos is composed of Varieties.[2] There are many substances and they are capable of repetition and *kinesis*

---

[1] On the complexity of Ornamentalist Humanism, see the 1st Ornamentalist Program, *Cosmos as Public Park*.

[2] We hold this position contra the monist or monist-tending doctrines of many who are nonetheless our collaborators: much of Speculative Realism and Object-Oriented Ontology; Whitman, Simondon, Deleuze, Bergson, Whitehead, Charles Olson, Robert Duncan, Jane Bennett, Guido Cavalcanti.

(with the help of the logic and syntax of decoration we have thus worked out the dilemmas of the Pre-Socratics and perhaps averted philosophy). Phenomenology is generalizable to every thing and appearance need not be appearance for-me. Things appear to each other to the extent that they appear as mutually ornamental. So difference remains and ontology matters; ethics remains ethics only when thought from difference, and even the conservation of matter and energy (Whitmanic or scientific) will never quell our grief or lead us to arrogance (that amnesia of finitude that leads to instrumentalization). Variation determines the logics, syntax, ontology, and rhetoric of ornament.

B1.

Cosmos is the space-time of the actual. The great architect Gottfried Semper teaches us that ornament is not inessential to shelter. Reading Semper, Maker Lisa Robertson explicates ornament as the elaboration of surface, the production of variation of surface that multiplies affect. Through ornament, "affect invades the center."[3] We would extend the definition of surface to any attribute of a being that does not strictly coincide with the ontology of its three-dimensionality; and we would extend the operation of ornament to inter-phenomenal interface and a softening of the MONAD (increase of interest→"affect"→ intensification of interface). Ornament as event of differentiation and as antidote to instrumentality.

C.

"History" as surface. Poesis as decoration. Serious medievalism as a particularly inflected poetics of decorating temporal and historical surfaces. It is no insult to say that

---

[3] Lisa Robertson, "*Rubus Armeniacus:* A Common Architectural Motif in the Temperate Mesophytic Region," in *Occasional Work and Seven Walks from the Office for Soft Architecture* (Toronto: Coach House, 2011), 111–112.

medievalists are to be kept around for ornamental purposes.[4] Ornament constructs provisional phenomenological pavilions, and articulations of difference as ground for both ethics and hospitable sheltered interfaces. Medieval studies must make ornaments of, with, and for, the medieval, elaborating that bolt of fabric we call the medieval into interface with cosmos in the present.

D.

We need provisional medievalist gems; for example: newly analog Records, flexible and adorned with Wonder, *Chevalrie,* Brocade, Romance, *Ofermod,* Philology, and Sap.[5]

---

[4] Cf. Will Woodward and Rebecca Smithers, "Clarke Dismisses Medieval Historians," *The Guardian*, May 9, 2003, http://gu.com/p/jvzg.

[5] Addendum to clarify certain negative positions in light of the affirmative tone of the above: we oppose capitalism and the state; also fossil fuels, archic governance and its puppet "representation," some computers, the so-called obsolescence of print, etc.

20/

A MEDIEVAL: MANIFESTO

Christopher Roman

A medieval refuses 'the.' 'The' indicates singularity, a reaching back to see a monolith. But, the Angel of History does not see the past as monolith; it approaches in fragments, pieces and chairs, bookcases and drops, reaching out with its queer touch.

A medieval does not rest. Once it has been identified it has already been lost. What is left is an event that is its becoming.

A medieval is evident in slime trails that are left. These paths ooze into the earth, evaporate into air. They are reflected in whatever light is shined upon them.

A medieval is that what you held when you said "that's just like the Wife of Bath" to your friend as you walked to a snow-covered car, and she was telling tales about her second husband and his inability to get his ass off the couch. She owned those red stockings.

A medieval is dust.

A medieval is that trace left at the midnight showing of *The Hobbit* and you thought "this is a movie of the archive." This is the unearthed, turned over, violent, non-faithful version. And, you were conflicted, and you went to see it again the next day.

A medieval is that thing you thought you focused on only to realize the marginalia taunting you with a horn up its ass.

A medieval is the moment you realized the university was the reified monument of architectural stasis. And, you, you were Abelard without his balls, and you realized you had to move, you had to make a Paraclete. A university depended on it.

A medieval is Sir Gowther. It is an instant when you realize breeding doesn't matter—you razed that village, you "sowyked hom so thei lost ther lyvys."[1] You made sure those too-rooted institutions burned to the ground. You were forgiven. You built them again.

A medieval is a realization that if you sleep under a tree you will rise up with ghosts or elves or demons or your mother.

A medieval is the refusal of the exploitation of labor and recognizing there is no outside of capital.

---

[1] *Sir Gowther*, in *The Middle English Breton Lays*, ed. Anne Laskaya and Eve Salisbury (TEAMS: Kalamazoo, MI, 2001), 113.

A medieval is seeing without your eyes.

A medieval is the palimpsest that is your heart—one layer is blood, another animal skin, another light, and beneath that ... and beneath that ... and beneath that.

A medieval is neither terminus nor origin.

A medieval is the polyphony of the angel, music no one hears.

A medieval prehends, revealing unknown surfaces, illuminating interiors, leaving traces.

A medieval is not bound by transcendent time; rather it produces time in its relations with objects.

A medieval is how you found your power by standing in the river. They are throwing axes at you; they are piercing your skin. You are not falling down.

A medieval is my failed wings: "se non che la mia mente fu percossa / da un fulgore in che sua voglia venne."[2]

A medieval is your contemplation of finitude. It is where time, book, flesh meet at that instant only to reveal expanse that is immanently eternal.

A medieval is our work.

---

[2] Dante, *Paradiso*, eds. and trans. Robert Hollander and Jean Hollander (New York: Anchor Books, 2007), XXXIII, 140–141.

21/

HOMO NARRANS

Eva von Contzen

My title is borrowed from a book by John D. Niles on the pervasiveness of storytelling among human beings.[1] Niles investigates oral literature from both an anthropological and a cultural perspective and demonstrates its socio-cultural grounding and significance. We think in stories and narrativize our experiences in the world. We transform objects, natural processes, and unrelated occurrences into narratives by establishing links of coherence and causality, by adding personification and anthropomorphism, and by projecting feelings onto that which surrounds us. We tell stories to soothe, to debate, to invite response, to strengthen friendship, to remember, to argue,

---

[1] John D. Niles, *Homo Narrans: The Poetics and Anthropology of Oral Literature* (Philadelphia: University of Pennsylvania Press, 2010).

to bond, and to define our identity—the list could be extended endlessly, so manifold are the reasons and motivations behind the storytelling impulse.

Within medieval studies, I have the impression we have neglected, even lost our interest in literature as narratives and have replaced it with trusting our own powers of creating narratives instead. The broadening of the field towards new and without doubt exciting theoretical approaches, such as object-oriented criticism, and the ever-growing influence of internet-based methods and forms of communication, create new narratives, about people, concepts, objects, and discourses, resulting in a narrativization of narratives. Despite our concern about critique and our awareness of our methods and scholarly distance, I believe we need to be much more conscious about both medieval narratives and processes of narrativization and our own input and interpretation of them.

Hence my rant is about what I perceive to be a general neglect of the parameters of medieval narratives and the processes that create, underlie, and fuel them. Niles's term *homo narrans* is deliberately modelled upon the term *homo sapiens* and suggests, quite rightly so, the anthropological constant of the concept, which links our postmodern society with pre-modern people and thinking. Back to the narratives! This does not mean that I proclaim a return to close reading in the worst kind of narrowness and the exclusion of any form of context, nor that I am in fervent favour of either structuralism or surface reading. On the contrary: I think a return to the narratives should focus on the *strategies* of narrativization, their processual, dynamic, flexible, fluid, dialogic elements, in other words, what makes them narratives in relation to the poets' self-understanding, the contexts of the stories, their intertextualities, their engagement of the audience as well as their impact, functions, and potential of creating affectivity. A.C. Spearing, among others, has recently made very interesting suggestions about reading medieval first-person narratives, readings that I find highly suggestive and which shed new light on how to read the 'I' in medieval texts.[2] At the same time, I see a danger in applying meta-narrative readings, of which Franco Moretti's study *Graphs, Maps, Trees: Abstract Models for a Literary History* is a prime example.[3] Moretti attempts to narrativize literary history using as his narrative form abstract models borrowed from statistics. Yet his graphs in no way do justice to the complexities of a history of narratives; they even suppress it, and reduce literature to non-narratives, to abstractions that make literary scholars unnecessary and rob us of our sources. Maybe the Middle Ages as a period are un-narratable as a whole because they are so varied, and because manuscript culture does not allow for the one story to be told—but for a variety of plots that demonstrate a pervasive stability and come in many disguises.

Am I proclaiming a paradigm shift towards narrative? Yes, because I believe a new focus on narrative and narrativization would enable us to discover medieval literature anew so that the ostensibly known and familiar can acquire a new alterity, which subsequently becomes a new familiarity, thus transforming the texts by what may be their most basic aspect: the fact that they tell stories. Of course such a focus on narratives and narrativization requires the inclusion of and reliance on the many theories and approaches available, which can be brought into a happy union. Perhaps the post-postmodernist period can be heralded by the return to the narrative and the rediscovery of narration as the fundamental force of literature.

---

[2] A.C. Spearing, *Medieval Autographies: The 'I' of the Text* (Notre Dame: University of Notre Dame Press, 2012) and *Textual Subjectivity: The Encoding of Subjectivity in Medieval Narrative and Lyric* (Oxford, UK: Oxford University Press, 2005).
[3] Franco Moretti, *Graphs, Maps, Trees: Abstract Models for a Literary History* (London: Verso, 2005).

22/

HISTORICISM AND ITS DISCONTENTS

Erik Wade

A text is being historicized. As with Freud's famous essay on the fantasy "a child is being beaten," what matters most is the fantasy that the vague statement covers over.[1] What is the fantasy that historicism supports? Numerous arguments have been raised against historicism.[2] Howev-

---

[1] Sigmund Freud, "A Child is Being Beaten: A Contribution to the Study of the Origin of Sexual Perversions," in Vol. 17 of *The Standard Edition of the Complete Psychological Works*, ed. and trans. James Strachey (London: Hogarth, 1953–74).
[2] A complete discussion of such critiques would be difficult to summarize, but a partial list might include Joan Copjec's *Read My Desire: Lacan Against the Historicists* (Cambridge, MA: MIT Press, 1994), Christopher Lane's work, as well as specifically medieval scholarship such as Aranye Fradenburg's *Sacrifice Your Desire: Psychoanalysis, Historicism, Chaucer* (Minneapolis: Uni-

er, my interest here lies less in those arguments than in exploring the fantasy that undergirds both historicism as well as its renunciation. What might it mean to give up historicism? Moreover, what might it mean to abandon a practice, as opposed to abandoning an object? This essay troubles the idea of letting go of historicism by suggesting that historicism is itself a kind of letting go, a relinquishing of the historical object to a distant past. So, to let go of historicism is to refuse to let go of the historical object. This refusal, however, remains obscured and unacknowledged beneath a fantasy of historicism's historicity.

In order to set up this kind of thought experiment, I will use the psychoanalytic concepts of mourning and melancholia as a way to explore the fantasy of historicism. The two processes (i.e., mourning and historicism) are not the same. However, it may be productive to see what is gained by understanding historicism as a kind of mourning, a way of mourning and of letting go of the historical object (be it text, artifact, person, culture, or event). I mean "mourning" precisely in the sense of Freud's *Mourning and Melancholia*: mourning is what Freud thought was the correct psychic process, in which we let go of the lost love-object and *get over it*. Perhaps historicism is an attempt to *get over* those texts from the distant past, to remove their surprising, anxiety-producing, traumatic connotations in favor of something that affected people— once—in a time that is now passed. After all, historicism asks us to try to understand how a previous culture might have experienced, understood, and felt about an object. To summarize briefly: historicism imagines that the text was once known by a past culture and thus can be explained by situating it within that previous culture.[3] It

---

versity of Minnesota Press, 2002) or Amy Hollywood's work.

[3] When I speak about "historicism," I am a little imprecise, partially because I feel that the average use of "historicism" is often imprecise. Furthermore, as many have noted, people often cited as New Historicists frequently rejected the label themselves, leaving New Historicism proper with little in the way of a truly agreed-upon methodology. Larry Scanlon notes that criticisms

imagines that such a text is unsurprising, because any surprises it might give us today result from our estrangement from it as modern readers unable to access the past fully. By rejecting grand narratives for localized knowledge and by rejecting alternate ways of knowing a text, historicism (in its most excessive forms) limits both how we might talk about a text and our ability to imagine how a text might remain startling to its cultural milieu. By recovering the past while insisting on its alterity, historicism is always in danger of "getting over" the past through rendering it safe and unsurprising. This is not Freud's melancholia, where we never get over the text, and it never fails to trouble us. This is mourning, where the text can be made sense of and released. The past, historicism often insists, is dead and no longer with us.

In doing this, the fantasy of historicism is that we can understand the historical object in relation to the other

---

of New Historicism often fail to distinguish between it and the older forms of historicism (which increasingly are resurfacing and replacing the more theoretical style of New Historicism): Larry Scanlon, "Historicism: Six Theses," *postmedieval FORUM* 1 (October 2011): http://postmedieval-forum.com/forums/forum-i-responses-to-paul-strohm/scanlon/. It is my suspicion that some criticisms of "historicism" often take the form of claims very similar to those that might be forwarded by New Historicists. For instance, in a retrospective essay about New Historicism, Catherine Gallagher and Stephen Greenblatt comment that "[the New Historicist notion of a distinct, local culture as a text] carries that core hermeneutic presumption that one can occupy a position from which one can discover meanings that those who left traces of themselves could not have articulated": Catherine Gallagher and Stephen Greenblatt. *Practicing New Historicism*. (Chicago: The University of Chicago Press, 2000), 8. Aranye Fradenburg, arguing against historicist methodologies, suggests that instead, "We cannot confine the work of knowing the Middle Ages to replicating, however hopelessly and/or heroically, medieval cultures' self-understandings" (L.O. Aranye Fradenburg, *Sacrifice Your Love*, 77). Both arguments—for a methodology that produces knowledge that the culture did not have—are suggestive of possible similarities despite remaining ranged on either side of the psychoanalysis/historicism debate.

coordinates of the historical moment, which are always already known. The object is always *unsurprising*. As Larry Scanlon argues, historicism places itself in the bind of imagining that the historical object must always be within the range of the possibilities of the cultural moment. In his words, this "implicitly declares that the author or text in question has nothing to teach us."[4] This can even lead to the assumption that the text had nothing to teach its historical moment. Moreover, historicism implies that context determines text completely. Like biographical criticism, historicism suggests that all aspects of the text can be explained through recourse to a master text, whether that master text is the author or the surrounding culture. Some suggest that non-historicist practices flatten out historical difference between the Middle Ages and the present by imagining continuity between past and present. However, *historicism is not historical enough*. Through its fantasy of a safely knowable, self-contained past, historicism is often in danger of flattening out historical difference within the Middle Ages itself: as Scanlon notes, it makes "medieval culture all center with no margin."[5]

The fantasy of historicism is a fantasy that one can in fact know the object. Both Slavoj Žižek and Joan Copjec argue that historicizing serves to pass over or foreclose the traumatic Real of a particular moment, what Žižek calls the fundamental social antagonism or what Copjec calls the anxiety of the overproximity of the Real.[6] Certainly, untheorized historicism often serves the precise function of placing the historical object at a remove from

---

[4] Larry Scanlon, "Historicism: Six Theses."
[5] Larry Scanlon, "Historicism: Six Theses."
[6] Copjec, *Read My Desire*, particularly her chapter "Vampires, Breast-feeding, and Anxiety." Žižek has made versions of this argument (between psychoanalysis and historicism, psychoanalysis and constructivism, and psychoanalysis and contingency) in many publications. His collaborative volume with Judith Butler and Ernesto Laclau is a useful start: Judith Butler, Ernesto Laclau, and Slavoj Žižek, *Contingency, Hegemony, Universality: Contemporary Dialogues on the Left* (New York: Verso, 2000).

us, of protecting from its becoming uncomfortably close to our moment. We fantasize that we have the capacity to understand the culture that produced the object, and we often yearn to see the object as 'representative' of its time—even as representative of the "medieval mind"—and as always at a historical distance, enclosed in its own historical episteme: the worldview shifts so completely from period to period that continuity does not exist. The society of torture and punishment and public spectacle that Foucault has seen as so characteristic of the Middle Ages seems wholly alien from the panoptic society of prisons and disciplines that arose shortly after it.[7] The coordinates of truth and knowledge appear to have shifted entirely. Thus, from the historicist's point of view, no object from this other era could possibly have historical weight for us in the contemporary era. The moats of epistemic shift prevent it.

This is, of course, an extreme view of historicism, but it is a fantasy that nonetheless remains potent for many fields of medieval criticism, such as identity studies. A lack of historical continuity allows historicists to object that considering race, gender, or sexuality in the Middle Ages is an anachronistic imposition of a modern view on a medieval text.

This practice of explaining the historical object and of distancing it from ourselves functions as an analogue to Freud's idea of mourning. We might feel in this interest a desire to always postpone the moment when we consider how we might understand the object, or how we do, or how we will, or how we may never. All of these feelings, I suggest, are foreclosed and held at bay by the mourning of historicism for this object, a mourning that allows (in fact requires) that the object be let go and consigned to a knowable past.

If the issues I have sketched out are indeed valid problems with historicism, then how might we let go of historicism as a practice? *Should* we let go of historicism

---

[7] Michel Foucault, *Discipline and Punish: The Birth of the Prison*, trans. Alan Sheridan (New York: Vintage Books, 1995).

and work to get over it? We might refuse to get over the historical object, by refusing to mourn it and leave it for dead in the distant past. We might refuse the fantasy of a text whose range of meanings is exhausted by its historical context and that is always unsurprising. *The Canterbury Tales* remain surprising despite knowing their cultural and historical context. Perhaps they are even sometimes surprising *because* I know that context. This refusal to mourn is a refusal not to be surprised or moved or indebted. As Sara Ahmed has commented in her work on queer grief, "to preserve an attachment is not to make an external other internal, *but to keep one's impressions alive, as aspects of one's self that are both oneself and more than oneself, as a sign of one's debt to others.*"[8]

I follow theorists like Copjec in imagining that giving up (or reining in) historicism's excesses does not mean refusing historicity. By delivering the text over to a certain unknowability, by allowing it to retain its powerful, dramatic, surprising presence, one allows it to exist as a rupture or change in the period around it, as a series of brackets containing something that may be new or old or both or neither. Nevertheless, we need not imagine that historicism must be let go entirely. Perhaps as scholars we ought simply to inhabit the tension between present readings (possibly just allowing themselves to be surprised by texts) and historicist foreclosures of meaning (which attend to cultural context). We must imagine a historicity that need not let go of—nor mourn—history and its objects.[9]

---

[8] Sara Ahmed, *The Cultural Politics of Emotion* (Edinburgh: Edinburgh University Press, 2004), 160.

[9] I would like to thank Stacy Klein and Pamela Wolpert for their comments and suggestions on the paper. I would also like to thank the audience at the BABEL Working Group panel, "Fuck This: On Finally Letting Go," held at the 2012 Kalamazoo Congress on Medieval Studies, where I delivered an earlier version of this paper, for their questions and comments.

23/

'TIS MAGICK, MAGICK THAT WILL HAVE RAVISHED ME

Lisa Weston

Medievalists, especially philologists like me—and perhaps like some of you as well—we play with dead things. Within the late capitalist, utilitarian, increasingly techno-bureaucratic and determinedly non-magical University, our fondness for the impractical arts and humanities and such, our philological and historical pursuits may well appear an unseemly (or at least useless) preoccupation with the past, a *philia* (or paraphilia) for "dead" languages and cultures. Necrophilia, not to put too fine a point on it. But in the face of such institutional abjection, let us not surrender our *philia* so much as transform it—into *mantia*. Let us (re)claim and reconstruct our engagement with the "dead" as necromancy—from the Latin *necromantia*, borrowed in turn from post-Classical Greek νεκρομαντεια (*nekromanteía*), from νεκρος (*nekrós*) "dead body" and μαντεια (*manteía*) "prophecy or divination"—the discovery of hidden knowledge and especially the prediction or perhaps rather creation of the future through intercourse (pun intended) with the "dead" past.

Once upon a time, *grammar*, the study of texts, especially those written in that archetypical "dead" language, Latin, was synonymous with even as it was linguistically related to *grimoire*, a particular kind of text, a manual of physical talismans, charms and ritual performances of summoning, commanding and banishing supernatural entities. In fourteenth and fifteenth century Scots, indeed, the one loan-word *gramarye* (from the Old French *grammaire*) encompassed both grammar (learning in general) and magic (occult learning in particular), and also gave us the associated *glamour,* both noun and a verb. And glamour, one must admit, is a quality sadly lacking from many plans to save the humanities by making them more obviously practical and useful. This, then, is a manifesto—and I use that word, too, as both noun and verb—to manifest magical, fantastical and eccentric glamour in our scholarship and teaching.

Ah, as Chaucer wrote, those "yonge clerkes that been lykerous / To redden artes that been curious" (*Franklin's Tale*, 1119-1120).[1] If his Clerk of Oxenford (like most of us) "al be that he was a philosopher," has little gold (alchemically or otherwise produced) in his coffer (*General Prologue* 297), hende Nicholas cynically (and practically) uses university students' reputation as necromancers who pry into "Goddes pryvetee" (*Miller's Tale* 3454) to gull his landlord. Yet we may imagine either or both of them passing by "Friar Bacon's study" on Folly Bridge. The Oxford scholar-magician Roger Bacon (c.1214–1294), *doctor mirabilis*, known for his magically-powered divinatory brazen head as much as for his works on optics, astronomy, and mathematics, stands a historical model for liter-

---

[1] All references to Chaucer's *Canterbury Tales* works from *The Riverside Chaucer,* gen. ed. Larry D. Benson, 3rd edn. (Boston: Houghton Mifflin, 1987), cited by title and line number.

ary masters of illusion and natural magic like Chaucer's clerk of Orleans, whose book "spak muchel of the operaciouns / Touchynge the eighte and twenty mansiouns / That longen to the moone" (*Franklin's Tale* 1129–1131).

Such books—grimoires—constitute a specific textual form, compendia of astral or angelic magic (that is, the discernment and invocation of celestial powers into talismans), like the thirteenth-century *Picatrix* (a translation of the twelfth-century Arabic *Ghâyat al-Hakîm fi'l-sihr*) or the *Liber Razielis Archangeli* (a translation of the Hebrew *Sefer Raziel Ha-Malakh*). Marsilio Ficino's 1471 translation into Latin of the ancient *Corpus hermeticum* represents a more recognizably humanist/philological intervention into the grimoire tradition, as do Heinrich Cornelius Agrippa's 1533 *Three Books of Occult Philosophy* and Giambattista Della Porta's 1558 *Magia Naturalis*. John Dee's 1564 *Monas Hieroglyphica*—Dee offers one likely contemporary model for Christopher Marlowe's 1592 *Doctor Faustus*, from which I borrow my title—drew on his experiments in angelic communication to create a still enigmatic treatise on symbolic language. Following upon the work of figures like Nostradamus (1503–1556) and Nicholas Flamel (1330–1418), whose *Livre des figures hiéroglyphiques* was published in London in 1624 as *Exposition of the Hieroglyphical Figures*, Dee attempted through his philological exploration to unify linguistics and alchemy, astronomy, music, and optics into one systematic theory of *logos*.

Severed from grimoire, however, grammar was transformed during the more positivist seventeenth and eighteenth centuries through the application of a more determinedly scientific method. In the developing disciplines of historical linguistics and the scientific study of mythology and religion, the magic of the past became a legitimate object of inquiry, perhaps, but no longer a present method. As grammar marched toward our present—and away from a necromantic past—grimoires moved into their own occult underworld. The 1670 publication in Paris of *the Grand Grimoire* spawned numerous revisions and analogues in an Enlightenment world that also included the Rosicrucians, Cagliostro (1743–1795 or maybe later, if he really was immortal) and Franz Mesmer (1734–1815). The word *grimoire* entered general English usage, in fact, after the 1801 publication of Francis Barrett's *The Magus*.[2] In the nineteenth century a somewhat more populist spiritualism—séances and spirit mediums—offered a less speculative, more mundane, even bourgeois belief-system, even as psychical phenomenon became the object of (para)scientific investigation. Although the practices and preoccupations of members of the Hermetic Order of the Golden Dawn, for example, and other elements of an occult underworld could still influence bohemian culture, especially the Symbolists and Surrealists, necromancy proper (as it were) remained the province of a few ceremonial or ritual magicians. From this tradition emerge the occult treatises of the infamous Aleister Crowley (1875–1947) and visionary-artist Austin Osman Spare, (1886–1956), who introduced his modern doctrine of sigils in his 1913 *Book of Pleasure*. Their theoretical experimental model for magical ritual greatly influenced later twentieth and twenty-first century Chaos Magic, especially as it appears in works like Peter J. Carroll's 1978 *Liber Null* and his later *Psychonaut* and *Psybermagick,* both originally published in 1995 and revised and expanded in 2007, and Patrick Dunn's 2008 *Magic Power Language Symbol*, a text very much in the spirit of John Dee's work on angelic language.

Although I am not (exactly or at least literally) calling for Freshman Composition to be replaced with Spellcasting, I maintain that there is much we can gain from reconnecting *grammar* and *grimoire*. As Christopher Lehrich argues, magic—magick in the tradition of Dee and the Golden Dawn—constitutes a theoretical mode that is good to think with, especially in its ability to sub-

---

[2] It was followed soon after by *The Grand Oracle of Heaven, or, the Art of Divine Magic* by Barrett's pupil John Parkin. Robert Cross Smith's 1822 *Philosophical Merlin* and 1825 *The Astrologer of the Nineteenth Century* did not sell well, however.

vert normative concepts: reason, truth and nature.[3] Anthropologist Barbara Tedlock, too, who defines divination as "a form of intentional shared social action" deriving a consensus reality through a dialogue between intuition and reason as the metaphors generated in visionary or mantic experience are ordered, sequenced and parsed, asks us to remember that the ancient Greek *theoria*, from which we derive our word *theory*, originally referred to a divinatory practice, to a sacred pilgrimage in search of knowledge: theorizing then entailed a journey to a distant land (or at least a scholarly conference?) or the divinatory combination of "the observation of material things seen in the physical world with a heightened form of witnessing, a sacramental form of seeing."[4] For Tedlock, diviners are "specialists who use the idea of moving from a boundless to a bounded realm of existence. They excel in insight, imagination, fluency in language and knowledge of cultural traditions. They construct useable knowledge from oracular messages by combining intuitive-synthetic modes of thinking with logical-analytic modes of thinking. Through a dialogical and interactive mode, they link diverse domains of representational information and symbolism with emotional or presentational experience."[5] That is, they deal in metaphor and construct more meaningful "realities" through rituals that are, at base, linguistic performances.

Despite the current fetishizing of data-driven analysis and observable, reproducible facts, scientists today imagine any number of things that defy positivist common sense: parallel universes, quantum non-locality, worm

---

[3] Christopher Lehrich, *The Occult Mind: Magic in Theory and Practice* (Ithaca: Cornell University Press, 2008).
[4] Barbara Tedlock, "Towards a Theory of Divinatory Practice," *Anthropology of Consciousness* 17.2 (2006): 67 [62–77]. See also her "Divination as a Way of Knowing: Embodiment, Visualization, Narrative, and Interpretation," *Folklore* 112 (2001): 189–197.
[5] Barbara Tedlock, "Theorizing Divinatory Acts: The Integrative Discourse of Dream Oracles," in *Divination: Perspectives for a new Millennium*, ed. Patrick Curry (Aldershot: Ashgate, 2010), 21 [11–23].

holes in time and space, particles that are also waves, or vice versa, depending on the observer. The universe of contemporary quantum physics is ever more a universe—one among a potentially infinite number in a multiverse—that is both inevitable, in that it does exist, and yet incapable of being deduced from scientific law, if not in fact impossible. For some physicists, indeed, our impossibly vibrant universe exists precisely because of and through our participation in its creation and contemplation. As Bob Tubshaw has argued recently, "in recent decades there has been growing recognition that cause and effect in human actions and human society are best interpreted through 'complexity theory' ('chaos theory' as it used to be called) and not through the more positivistic analyses that, although they may construct acceptable narratives in retrospect, offer little in the way of prediction. So if we see causality as a social construction . . . then divination takes its place as a subset of revised ontology of causality." Trubshaw in fact suggests that academic researchers take seriously the "sleight of mind" through which chaos magicians sometimes seek to "create a blurring of past, present, and future so that aleatory portents can be interpreted in ways that have meaning and significance."[6]

Language and the future—and the ways in which language constructs, deconstructs, reconstructs past, present and future, not necessarily in that order—are matters too important to leave in the care of those who would restrict their study to the utilitarian expression of "objective" truths—if physics indeed allows us that any more—marshaled toward explanations of how what "was" became what "is" (that is, what "must" be). I propose, rather, a necromantic humanities that "predicts" by creating from speculative imagined pasts desirable futures not required as inevitable reproductions of the present. Such a humanities would differ from the humanities of the present and positivist past by constituting itself not a

---

[6] Review of *Divination: Perspectives for a New Millennium* (Patrick Curry, ed.), in *Time and Mind: The Journal of Archaeology, Consciousness and Culture* 5.2 (2012): 219, 220 [217–220].

discipline so much as an orientation.

And to that end, I invoke—manifesto—scholars joyfully anarchic, outlaw, contrarian, and excessive, who embody all the ways our philosophies and philologies, our *philia,* should be about joy and not (just) utility. Manifesto humanities scholars who remember that the mythic word- and culture-creators like Hermes or Oðin were tricksters and magicians. Manifesto scholars who, like Chaos magicians, base their "pathworkings" and magical experiments in the worlds of *Star Trek* or *Doctor Who* or the Cthulu mythos, and who work through fabulation and visionary creation as much as through "scientific" analysis. Manifesto scholars who playfully take as models not only historical philologists but also the fictional scholar heroes of M.R. James's *Ghost Stories of an Antiquary,* magician-scholar-heroes like William Hope Hodgeson's Carnaki the Ghost Finder, Algernon Blackwood's John Silence, and Dion Fortune's Doctor Taverner. Not forgetting, of course, H.P. Lovecraft's scholar-adventurers, Charles Dexter Ward, Randolph Carter, and Henry Armitage, librarian of Miskatonic University and keeper of the fatal *Necronomicon.*

Manifesto, in sum, a humanities that will charm and glamour the future pasts and past futures we desire and will in our present. Our focus need not be "what was"—or at least on the creation of narratives that could account for and validate the present. We can, rather, learn from Chaos magicians as much as from physics that "we inhabit a tautological time of our own making," in which we forget that "entropy increases with time simply because we measure time in the direction in which entropy increases."[7] We can look at once backward and forward, retro-futuristically, to multiple possible futures through reconsideration of multiple possible pasts. We can practice sleight of mind, disdaining simple distinctions between "is" and "was" that render the past "dead," irreparably anterior and distinct from the present, let alone the

---

[7] Peter J. Carroll, *Psybermagick: Advanced Ideas in Chaos Magic* (Tempe, AZ: Original Falcon Press, 2008 [1995]), 94.

future. We can prefer instead more complex, messy tenses like the future past.

So mote it be: MANIFESTO.

BURN AFTER READING

Volume 2
The Future We Want:
A Collaboration

PREFATORY NOTE

THE FUTURE WE WANT

Jeffrey Jerome Cohen

The experimental essays gathered here had their origin in performance at the 48th International Congress of Medieval Studies in Kalamazoo, Michigan (May, 2013). The idea of this twelve-way collaboration was dreamed through a series of emails exchanged among Jonathan Hsy, Lowell Duckert, Eileen Joy, and Jeffrey Cohen. We set as our task imagining collective modes for contemplating how to shape the humanities, as well as the communities to which we belong at many levels, to bring about a future more our own, while wondering all the while how that first-person plural comes into being. Building upon a series of sessions at the previous year's Congress that had focused on the active engagement to which humanists must commit in order not to find themselves in merely passive, reactive, protest-oriented positions within their home institutions as well as at the many other homes we inhabit through daily acts of creation, we hoped to extend and intensify a conversation about how to shape the humanities, and ourselves, in the years ahead. We knew from the start that any such intervention had to be fully collaborative. Changing the world is not a solo project. But the working out of how such alliance and enmeshing might proceed was left to the participants.

"The Future We Want" was sponsored by the George Washington University Medieval and Early Modern Studies Institute (GW MEMSI). We would like to thank Elizabeth Teviotdale for her support of the endeavor, and for assisting us in finding a creative way to enable such a crowd of collaborators to appear in the session. The magnificent Eileen Joy has ensured that this project, like all Oliphaunt endeavors, has a welcoming home at punctum books. We also thank the audience who came that day and filled the auditorium with energy, enthusiasm, and difficult questions. The intervention did not work: the humanities are still, unfortunately, in crisis. But we have not given up, and we hope that you will now join us as collaborators and bring this work in whatever creative, new directions you are inspired to imagine as you dream the future you want.

Jeffrey Jerome Cohen
George Washington University

FIELD CHANGE/
DISCIPLINE CHANGE

Anne F. Harris and Karen Eileen Overbey

We want a collective future.

This is a material moment, and we want a material future. A *lush* future, a future of exploded views and inner lives of objects, a future of abundant encounters with the material and natural worlds, a future of touching objects that touch us back. A collective future, a collaboration with *things*.

We want to call out, through the discipline of Art History, to the field of medieval studies, and, further, to the endeavor of the Humanities, in this material moment, when the *objects* of medieval studies are more than ever in our sights. We *need* a field change: a change in our field of view, our field of vision, our visual field. If we perceive differently, we will conceive differently. Objects have hurtled through history to get here, why keep them still now? In the flat ontology of the future we want, objects keep moving: through juxtaposition, association, attention.

This can be our project: articulations of objecthood; descriptions of the interconnectedness of things. The deep and vital networks and circulations and operations. The aesthetics of ontology.

What would that look like? In an art history of flat ontology, for a start, a classical or neoclassical ideal of beauty would not determine a hierarchy of objects, styles, representations, histories. Beauty would come from being, rather than from relativism. We could then take our time with surfaces and with substances, teasing out and amplifying the charm, the allure, of material. In the aesthetics of ontology all materials matter; all materials have our attention, we can attend to all materials. And so our aesthetics would enlarge our sense of 'beauty' to compass the revelation of the workings and beings of any artwork. Any object. Oh!

For some, there may be a fear that aesthetics is distance, that to aestheticize is to make distant, shimmering; to hold off, to gaze at and even evaluate, and so to separate, to distinguish ourselves from our objects. But this is perhaps a definition of 'aesthetics' beholden to 18th- and 19th-century philosophy, in which the arts inhabit a special realm, set off from 'regular' experience, distinct especially from the mundane, just beyond the reach of average perception; this is aesthetics entwined with morality, and with teleology. In the future we want, aesthetics is intimacy: beauty is close and possible and not rare; it makes us pay attention, displace ourselves, look at manuscript, cross, cup, toaster with possibility. This is an understanding of 'aesthetic' at once very medieval and very modern: resonant with Ian Bogost's book and essay series *Object Lessons*,[1] and also with Aquinas's "animated sensory pleasures (*animales delectationes*)," in which we take delight in our physical and mental interactions with objects.[2] In medieval thought, as Mary Carruthers explains, "'aesthetic' meant 'knowledge acquired through sensory experiences'", and while human-made artefacts did have special status, it was more like the "ludic play space recog-

---

[1] See http://objectsobjectsobjects.com.
[2] See Mary Carruthers, *The Experience of Beauty in the Middle Ages* (Oxford, UK: Oxford University Press, 2013), 70–71. Aquinas's discussion of these sensory pleasures appears in his commentary on Aristotle's *Nichomachean Ethics*, especially in Book 3; see Thomas Aquinas, *In decem libros Ethicorum Aristotelis ad Nicomachum expositio*, ed. R. M. Spiazzi (Turin: Marietti, 1934).

nized by modern anthropology and psychology" than like the distant realm of Enlightenment and Romantic aesthetics.[3]

And so our aesthetics inhabit this play space to engage sensation and knowledge, to pay attention to material possibility, to be intimate with objects. But in this intimacy, this attention, we must not occlude the alien differentness, the wonder and strangeness of the art object. That strangeness, its being-beyond-interpretation, is what entices us.

Figure 1. The Lothar Cross, jeweled side ("Front"), c. 1000, gold, gilt silver and gems over a wood core, 49.8 cm x 38.8 cm x 2.3 cm. Cathedral Treasury, Aachen, photo by Ann Münchnow, photo ©: Domkapitel Aachen.

Here, for example: a visual field, an object. The Lothar Cross, given by the Ottonian Emperor to the church at

---

[3] Carruthers, *The Experience of Beauty*, 17.

Aachen just before the year 1000 (Fig. 1). This luxe *crux gemmata* is 50 cm high, an oak core covered in gold and silver gilt sheets, encrusted with 102 gems and 35 pearls, and further decorated with gold filigree and cloisonné enamel. The Cross's splendid workmanship, expensive materials, and Ottonian patronage were certainly as important as its religious meaning when it was affixed to a tall pole and carried in the public drama of liturgical processions.[4] At the center of the cross, where we might expect to find an image of Christ, is a sardonyx Augustan cameo, which we could (and which we have) read in relation to tenth-century imperial ideologies, spolia, and appropriation. More of the stones here are reused Classical gems, perhaps chosen for their historic or semiotic valence: an amethyst carved with the Three Graces, an onyx lion. Now, though, in the intimate play of a materialist ontology, we propose to see the strangeness: not the sure ideology, but the hesitation; not the power but the plea. A jewel is rare and demanding, but it is the result of geological imperfections; a cross affirms splendor and power, but a cross also asks for intercession and salvation.

So we can change our field of vision, discipline ourselves to look more materially. When we look at the object, and not only at the image (*crux gemmata*, emperor, lion, *Romanitas*) we see that most stones were set to highlight their color and their size, their lush materiality; they play a visual rhythm along the four arms of the cross. Iridescent blue teardrops at each terminal, and at the base of each blue stone a pearl; paired green squares at the interior angles of the cross arms; two sets of double rows of symmetrical dots along the length, remarkably consistent in size and shape. We can start to trace the tendrils of the filigree, to think with the object: the delicate strands of beaded gold wire, laid curled and queued to breathe in the spaces between the gems. The effects of movement and depth when one tendril drapes across another. The barely-visible daubs of solder (gold, to be sure, but less pure, with a slightly different melting point to adhere the filigree to the plane of gold plate). The uneven edges of the bezels, tamped close around the gems with tiny hammers, or pressed by careful fingers.

---

[4] For excellent recent work on the Cross, see Eliza Garrison, *Ottonian Imperial Art and Portraiture: The Artistic Patronage of Otto III and Henry II* (Burlington: Ashgate, 2012).

To look more materially, at first, is to look more closely. A close looking, in pace with the close reading of a text. To look, if not innocently, then not all-knowingly, either. In an art history of flat ontology, we will seek the mundane within the rare: the point where the tendril of the filigree does not accomplish its curl, where the band around the gem is crooked, where the gesture-to-make became tedious, where the matter is predictable. Does this "humanize" the object? Make the gleaming gem susceptible to human faltering? Our ontology is flat, let's turn the table: human faltering gathers around a gleaming gem. An art history of flat ontology doesn't humanize the object, it collapses the rare into the mundane, it fuses human gesture with the object's becoming, the human's becoming (from emperor to museum director to viewer) with the object's gesture (the Lothar Cross processed thousands of times before it was stilled by the museum). Close looking doesn't reveal things to valorize them: it upends them, it disintegrates the whole for its parts, oscillating between present materiality, past gesture, future desire (see Fig. 2). At some point, in some way we want to attend to, the Lothar Cross is equally ordinary and extraordinary.

Figure 2. The Lothar Cross, oblique view of jewels and filigree. Cathdral Treasury, Aachen, photo ©: Domkapitel Aachen.

More closely, and from a shifted perspective, we see that the gem settings are architectonic, miniature domed drums and arcades, a tiny landscape evoking (perhaps) the splendor of the City of Heaven. Reading this way, iconographically, we take the Cross's surface in all at once; we take its meaning. But if we linger, if we luxuriate in that very medieval pleasure of the "multifocal perspective," we can feel the dizzying shifts of scale and illusion and distortion, the push and pull of "minificence and magnificence," the wonder of material play.[5] Here we falter, we fall, into what Ian Bogost might call the "native logic" of the object.[6]

Figure 3. The Lothar Cross, detail view of jewels and filigree. Cathdral Treasury, Aachen, photo ©: Domkapitel Aachen.

We look again (Fig. 3), letting the stones and gold lead us, both intimate and strange. We then notice that some

---

[5] On "minificence and magnificence," and the pleasures of puzzlement in medieval artefacts (both text and image), see Carruthers, *The Experience of Beauty*, 151–155, 172–175, and 187–193.
[6] Ian Bogost, *Alien Phenomenology, or What It's Like to Be a Thing* (Minneapolis: University of Minnesota Press, 2012).

stones are drilled for beading, perhaps once part of Byzantine jewelry; the gems engraved with figures of Roman gods or animals are set upside down or sideways, resisting figural readings.[7] The intention isn't towards meaning, it's towards form: that drilled pearl can no longer be seen for the necklace it might once have been a part of, now you see it for its luster in a new luxury, you see it in its own lushness. Symbolism-as-intention is tricky here, too, when we know that some of these stones are post-medieval replacements, and nineteenth-century repairs. This is an object that to some degree resists iconography and narratology, and so resists much of art history's modern methods. What does it mean for art history to think about meaning beyond a single or originary moment of creation, beyond a first, or second, reception? As we move away from that originary point of creation, meaning and being start to intersect in new ways. The meaning is no longer simply what the original maker or user intended; it will be what you intend, what you attend to. Being asserts itself over meaning: the Cross survived, the pearl clung on, it is here and *that* is the new starting point.

Materiality, as Michael Ann Holly writes, "is that which halts transparency."[8] It stops us seeing through, seeing past, the object to something else, to something beyond or besides. It keeps us focused, it slows us down and makes us play, gives us pleasure. We will rediscipline our eye to look more closely, more materially, to admit play and pleasure, and to *be moved* in and by the object.

So: our future is a shift in our field of vision, in the field of play for and with objects.

THE BOON AND BOTHER OF LUSHNESS

The field of play of art history has always been drawn by and to objects. You can see why.

---

[7] A recent study of these and other "misplaced" engraved stones is Genevra Kornbluth, "Roman Intaglios Oddly Set: the Transformative Power of the Metalwork Mount," in *'Gems of Heaven': Recent Research on Engraved Gemstones in Late Antiquity, c. AD 200-600*, eds. Chris Entwistle and Noël Adams, British Museum Research Publication 177 (London: Trustees of the British Museum, 2011), 248–256.

[8] Michael Ann Holly, in "Notes From the Field: Materiality," *Art Bulletin* 95 (2013): 16 [10–37].

Fantastic *things* whose materiality calls out. The responses of human interlocutors have never stopped changing, framed by liturgy, antiquarianism, connoisseurship, iconography, social history . . . , always carving out a new future they want with and from the objects. Every interpretive frame is a "future we want." The frame is how we now present our works of art to the future: the frame is now the means of transference, claiming ontological status for any object as art. The frame will change (always), but it will be there (always). The French and English Academies reveled in the frame: Poussin prized it, Derrida pried it open.[9] But think, now, of medieval works of art unbounded by frames, no means of transference save accident and personal desire, only indications (no certitudes) of meaning. *They don't exist.* And so we frame and re-frame medieval objects: with the medieval practices of liturgy and devotion, with the rarity of antiquarianism, with the knowing eye of connoisseurship, with the medieval texts that sustain iconography, with the political mission of social history. The future we want is the next frame, the frame of reference we can next share (and debate): feminism, sexuality, queer theory, post-colonialism, eco-criticism . . . . The frame is the object's network: we think we might dispense with it, get "back" to the "original" work, but any return is itself framed. Medieval texts are presented as the surest context, but materiality precedes and outlasts context: the gems pre-existed the cross by millions of years, and they will persist long after the cross has come undone. Frames (physical, digital, interpretive) are part of flat ontology—they are flattening agents. Different frames elicit different meanings, but let's consider how they shift *being*, too. Medieval objects are not immutable, their ontology can shift. It's how they got here in the first place: tree to wood to cross, mineral to suture to jewel. Let's hold on to the frame, let's keep making our means of transference to the object, let's keep the object moving, let's keep moving with the object.

---

[9] Paul Duro, *The Academy and the Limits of Painting in Seventeenth-Century France* (Cambridge, UK: Cambridge University Press, 1997). Duro discusses Poussin's letter to his friend Chantelou, in which the artist champions the use of the frame (180ff). Jacques Derrida, *The Truth in Painting*, trans. Geoff Bennington and Ian McLeod (Chicago: University of Chicago, 1987), especially "The Parergon," 37–82.

Object-oriented ontology creates a vigorous field of play, one that makes for optimistic declarations: one in which we can revel in the material agency of the object, in which we can turn to our objects and see them *do things*. What is a hammer when it's not hammering? What is a cross when it's not processing (or blessing or saving or frightening)? What is the *work* of art when it is not meaning something? It is gem pressed into gold, cameo found and reinserted; it *does* light and color, it embodies texture and rarity—it makes us want a future whose material possibility makes us gasp. Lurking under, hovering over, is a metaphor, a possibly dematerialized future, but for now the material holds us fast; we fasten it to a frame and hold on.

Lushness has been the boon and bother of art history, it is that aspect of materiality around which the field changes; material, form, luster, texture, gleam, color, illusion—lushness is one of the qualities we try to frame. It is feared (think of Bernard of Clairvaux fighting the allure of image). It is administered (think of Suger assuring himself that he was seeing *through* the gems). It is measured (formalisms, iconographies, semiotics . . . Commandments). The Calf, lest we forget, was golden. We try to control lush materiality, and our resulting pleasure. The pleasure that comes from gleam and color, touch and texture. Why is pleasure so unnerving? Why does it become an ethical dilemma? Is it because we are overwhelmed by the agency of the object in our moments of pleasure? Because wonder might be more about the force of the object than about our possession of it?

Bernard's aesthetic asceticism gives us one of the best description of the thrill of images, and the condemnation of pleasure from lushness. The sensual seduction and harsh sanctimoniousness of the *Apology* makes even the act of reading it an ethical exercise. He lets lushness languish in gorgeous word, sight and sound ("pulchre lucentia, canore mulcentia, suave olentia, dulce sapientia, tactu placentia") before calling it all shit ("ut stercora").[10]

---

[10] Bernard of Clairvaux, *Sancti Bernardi Opera, III, Tractatus et Opscula*, ed. J. Leclercq, H.-M. Rochais (Rome: Editions Cisterciennes, 1963): "we [monks like Bernard who] deem things that gleam with beauty, soothe with sound, please with smell, temper with sweetness, lighten with touch, as shit." Translation by Anne Harris.

What delight did Bernard take in stripping delight of its delightfulness? The question is put not in terms of vindictiveness, but rather, precisely, in terms of pleasure: his word play seizes on the material forms of language and makes them dance—"deformis formositas/formosa deformitas," quoth he. He dips his quill deep into the stuff of his words, tracing letters and shifting endings, before he seeks to abolish the materiality altogether. He knows his stuff: in detail and precision, he mocks color and texture and form, and he derides viewers' helpless attraction to beauty. Then he lowers the ethical hammer: "The church adorns her stones in gold, and abandons her naked sons."[11] You can feel chastened reading Bernard. Of course he's right: bread before baubles, food before fantasy. But who is he to tell anyone that their pleasure at beauty is empty? Who are we to do so? Or not do so? Thus, the dilemma.

But even Bernard can't stay in it too long, even Bernard needs resolution, frames: "Assentio," he says in response to Psalm 26:8's declaration, "Lord, I have loved the beauty of your house." He agrees that churches should be adorned, because the good that material opulence might do for the "simple and devout" outweighs the power it gives the "vain and avaricious." Appeal, pertinence, usefulness—those are Bernard's frames for lushness and they are still very much in use today to curtail or justify the beauty of materiality. You can be sympathetic to Bernard: he was overwrought at the lushness of wrought things because he understood their allure and agency. You can be aggravated with him: his attempts to strip lushness of its place in spirituality results in a moralization of beauty and form that creates hierarchies (monastic elites and devout simpletons) and divides. For us—for the future we want—these can be breached by the aesthetics of flat ontology.

Because the material will out: the wonder of Augustus's lush cameo freaks out the center of the Lothar cross. In the future we want, lushness is vibrant: it unnerves us with pleasure, it blurs the boundary of discipline and desire, it *acts* on us. We want this play, this field of riotous blooming, this fertility. We want to stay longer in the conundrum of lushness: its ability to nurture but not to feed,

---

[11] "Suos lapides induit auro, et suos filios nudos deserit."

how it moves us in its stillness. We want to consider Jane Bennett's "shift from epistemology to ontology."[12] The future we want is on a material trajectory of perpetual becoming, how objects come to be, how they are at any given time, and we with them.

STRUGGLES AT HAND: THE ETHICAL PROJECT OF ART HISTORY

This is a way of engaging a long history of (as Maura Nolan has recently written) sensation and aesthetics, from Augustine and Aquinas to Adorno and Elkins.[13] And in this project, texts should not be our only primary sources. Objects themselves, and art objects especially, in their very *made-ness*, their facture, in their uneasy difference from the natural world (even if that difference is only the frame, the setting of a pearl into a hammered gold bezel), disclose the depth and the varieties of human-object networks and assemblages.

In all this close looking, this luxuriating in lushness, this pleasure, beauty, and ekphrasis, we find ourselves taking up some rather old-fashioned art historical methods. And we find ourselves sympathetic to the demands of formalists and connoisseurs that we see artwork for itself. It's easy to see the affinity here: the artist and art critic Roger Fry (1866-1934), for example, championed the autonomy of the visual ecounter with art, apart from literary and historical knowledge, and described the specific formal elements of artworks— especially "plasticity"—that grip the viewer and provoke the aesthetic experience.[14] Giovanni Morelli (1816-1891), Bernard Berenson (1865-1959), and other connoisseurs wrote lovingly and persuasively of specific details of paintings and sculptures. Bernson even described the aesthetic experience as a loss of boundary between viewer and object:

> In visual art the aesthetic moment is that fleeting instant, so brief as to be almost timeless, when the

---

[12] Jane Bennett, *Vibrant Matter: A Political Ecology of Things* (Durham: Duke University Press, 2010), 3.
[13] Maura Nolan, "Medieval Sensation and Modern Aesthetics: Aquinas, Adorno, Chaucer," *Minnesota Review* 80 (2013): 145–158.
[14] See Roger Fry, *Transformations: Critical and Speculative Essays on Art* (London: Chatto & Windus, 1926), especially Chapter 1, "Some Questions in Esthetics," 1–44.

> spectator is at one with the work of art he is looking at . . . . He ceases to be his ordinary self, and the picture or building, statue, landscape, or aesthetic actuality is no longer outside himself. The two become one entity; time and space are abolished and the spectator is possessed by one awareness.[15]

And for Heinrich Wölfflin (1864-1945), art was a visual language, a distinct mode of knowledge: the agency of the work itself acted through formal and stylistic means.

Such possibility, in these ideas, for our materialist project, for the future we want! But we are uncomfortable, too, with this legacy. Because connoisseurship and nineteenth-century formalism wrought *command* of objects, and teleologies of style and masters. Because aesthetics was most often transhistorical and absolute. Uncomfortable because our opening to objectness and materiality and lushness seems also to reopen an old disciplinary wound, the tension between aesthetics and structuralism.[16]

And so this future that we want troubles us, and in realizing it we must attend to this tension: do we have to give up the care for the liberal democratic subject nurtured by the hermeneutic projects of iconography, feminism, marxism, and postcolonialism? Over the last forty or so years, by exploring how we know objects, by exploring their meaning, function, and use-value to patrons, makers, and beholders, art history described the workings of power and the inequities of representation. This has given us a political and ethical project in art history, one that we value, inhabit, and want to defend.

Can our lush object-oriented future be an ethical one, too?

---

[15] Bernard Berenson, *Aesthetics and History* (London: Constable, 1950), quoted in Michael Ann Holly, "The Melancholy Art," *Art Bulletin* 89.1 (2007): 7 [7–17].

[16] For a recent exploration of this divide, see Francis Halsall, "Making and Matching: Aesthetic Judgement and Art Historical Knowledge," *Journal of Art Historiography* 7 (2012): 1–17. The gap between personal, "subjective" writing about art and "traditional" art historical scholarship is perhaps nowhere more apparent than in T.J. Clark's lovely book, *The Sight of Death: An Experiment in Art Writing* (New Haven: Yale University Press, 2006), a meditation on his relationship with two paintings by Poussin.

To think about the ethics of beauty and materiality we can look not only to Bennett and Bogost and Harman and Latour, but also to our medieval objects-in-themselves, which had their own ethical power and moral presence. Medieval beholders knew, as we do, the power of art-objects to elevate the human spirit. So much of the medieval encounter with *things* was revelatory. Abbot Suger knew it when he wrote of the transformative power of precious stones:

> Thus, when—out of my delight in the beauty of the house of God—the loveliness of the many-colored gems has called me away from external cares, and worthy meditation has induced me to reflect, transferring that which is material to that which is immaterial, on the diversity of the sacred virtues: then it seems to me that I see myself dwelling, as it were, in some strange region of the universe which neither exists entirely in the slime of the earth nor entirely in the purity of Heaven; and that, by the grace of God, I can be transported from this inferior to that higher world in an anagogical manner.[17]

The mystics—Meister Eckhart, Henry Suso, Mechthild and Hadewijch and Margery Kempe—knew, too, that looking at objects (and touching them, stroking them, losing yourself to them) could save your soul. And all kinds of devout beholders kissed manuscripts, fondled statues, tucked tiny relics into their clothing and jewelry to keep them close, intimate. Medieval devotional objects, as Caroline Walker Bynum reminds us, are not merely symbols, indexes, or icons, but the immediate presence of the holy.[18] That presence was in relics, of course, but it was also palpable in things like gemstones, which were formed through mysterious cosmic processes, and often had celestial origins. Objects like the jewelled Lothar Cross were efficacious and miraculous *because* of their materiality, not despite it, and the encounter with them depended on the sensory experience. Medieval objects—at least, these

---

[17] *De administratione*, trans. Erwin Panofksy (Princeton: Princeton University Press, 1979), 63–65.
[18] See Caroline Walker Bynum, *Christian Materiality: An Essay on Religion in Late Medieval Europe* (New York: Zone Books, 2011), 101–121.

devotional objects—were not simply instrumentalized by medieval beholders, but were understood as essentially embedded in networks, in assemblages, of icon, human, divine, nature, and material.

Figure 4. Saxo-Norman Crucible, mid-11th to mid-12th century, ceramic; earthenware, H 78 mm; DM (rim) 103 mm. Museum of London #13175.

Yet we cannot account only for the religious objects and the devotional networks. If we are to take seriously an aesthetics of ontology, we can't limit our vision (or our pleasure) to religious objects any more than to a canon of "masterworks." If "beauty" is loosened from some of its Kantian disinterest—which tends to separate "art" from artefact and "beautiful" from utilitarian[19]—then we can grapple with a problem we love: what is beautiful about medieval objects beside/beyond/outside their religious

---

[19] A good discussion of this is Ivan Gaskell, "Beauty," in *Critical Terms for Art History*, ed. Robert S. Nelson and Richard Schiff (Chicago: University of Chicago Press, 2003), 267–280.

import? Sure: some of their particular materiality tugs at modern/postmodern notional beauty and visual pleasure. But there is also the beauty of *survival*. The impossibility of medieval objects, for us: the fascination of their very present ontology. The *Beowulf* manuscript in the fire, the Staffordshire Hoard underground, the Ghent altarpiece in a salt mine. That survival doesn't have to be unique: the Saxo-Norman crucible, the clay lamp, the cooking pot (see Fig. 4). The mundane survives, too. How to attend to *these* objects? We can think of thirsty throats, cold fingers, and hungry mouths—we can see the beauty in that survival, in the persistence of presence, long after usefulness is gone and purpose is moot.[20]

The aesthetics of ontology begin with materiality: we can *attend to* the material *at hand*. We can marvel at the emergence, manipulation, and survival of the clay. We can think about use, but in the stillness of the museum, presence prevails. The aesthetics of flat ontology see the lushness of the clay cup. Of course, flat does not mean equal: we are not seeking to valorize clay to claim it as gold. We *are* asking for attention, for a future that attends to the power of the material, whether it be clay or gold. If the fundamental tenet of identity politics, of the political project of historicism, is *visibility*, can we turn that to making objects—of all sorts—visible? Can we value that, alongside the recovery of the muted voices of female embroiderers, alongside the exposure of violence in racial or class representation? Can the aesthetic act of description be an ethical practice?

Because—oh!—*that* is the future we want: an ethical relationship with objects that still allows for lushness.

STRUGGLES AWAIT: IDENTITY POLITICS

Oh! *That* is the future we want: an ethical relationship with objects that still allows for lushness.

And so we ask: What to do with lushness and its attendant decadence? The problem with lushness is that, usually, someone owns the lush object and wields its power. But might *our* pleasure dislodge unique owner-

---

[20] The Museum of London's collection includes over 150 pieces of hand-shaped Anglo-Saxon and Early Medieval ceramic, many of them catalogued here: http://www.museumoflondon.org.uk/ceramics/pages/category.asp?cat_id=693&page=1.

ship? Is there an element of pleasure that *takes possession* of the object of pleasure? Do we mock Protestantism and Puritanism and their mistrust of the material world? Easy. Harder to mock Marx and class consciousness. Harder to make it "all right" to prioritize the lushness of the Lothar Cross when there's a starving pilgrim nearby. So let's not. People have their own materiality, which can be strategized as identity politics. We have to confront the anxiety about object oriented ontology and post-humanism and eco-criticism displacing/replacing human subjects. But it's the belief that we are autonomous subjects wielding dependent objects that we want to break down. We're going to have to let our guard down as we move towards the collective future we want. We're going to have let ourselves, and everybody else, feel pleasure, feel the power of pleasure. Moments of enjoyment can become moments of resistance to singular ownership and hierarchy.

Bogost points out that we've worked hard for a long time to articulate an ethical relationship to each other, and lately to animals and the environment.[21] But, as surrounded with things as we are, as encased in objects as we've become, we have just begun to articulate, and maybe *form*ulate, an ethical relationship with objects. We want to be provoked to articulate an ethical approach to things. To experience how actants (be they cross, gold, Lothar, pilgrim, or the memory of Augustus as a really great emperor) are the builders of the collective reality. Can you fight social injustice by loving the Lothar Cross? You can't do it *through* the Cross as an object; you have to give up on yourself as the wielder of stuff to make things right. But remember, start to see: the pilgrim does her own looking and savoring outside of what you think is right. Each viewer is an actant in the ever-shifting experience of lushness guided by material, sense, perception, and response. These precepts of the aesthetics of ontology precede, and perpetually recede from, the concerns of epistemology. They will not attend to iconography, liturgy, or symbolism. They will group around the pilgrim, feel her tiredness and warmth, her thirst and relief, the dryness of her hands as her fingers reach for the cool touch of the cross or the crucible. Gather with her in wonder. We, the art historians, the gathered here today, are the latest act-

---

[21] Bogost, *Alien Phenomenology*, 74.

ants in the trajectory of this Cross, we hurtle forth with it for a little while, building collectives along the way—that's the future we want.

—⚍—

Ultimately, our call for the future (of our field, our discipline, our humanities endeavor) is not simply for a return to "materiality," or a "new" materialism, in relation to specific representations or objects. It is rather a call to treat the *objects* of medieval studies (the artworks, the texts, the artefacts, the histories, the people) with compassion. To *see* them in their native logics, their strangeness, their ontological beauty. Materiality is not a trend or a fashion or a mode; it *is* an ethical system, and it should inform our collective future. That's the future we want.

PARADIGM CHANGE/
INSTITUTIONAL CHANGE

L.O. Aranye Fradenburg and Eileen A. Joy

for Michael O'Rourke

THE ARTS OF LIVING

We are in the midst of paradigm change, brought on by initiatives like biological systems theory, post-structuralism, James Gibson's theory of affordances,[1] and neuroplasticity. Top-down or prime-mover models of change have given way to principles of creative interactivity and causal parity, in which concentrations of forces and systemic elements continue to play significant roles, but only as parts of turbulent, non-totalizable assemblages. The findings of the genome project have put genetic determinism in doubt. Today's genes do not write the scripts of our lives; they are relatively passive elements in a complex field of biochemical interactions. Jesper Hoffmeyer summarizes the situa-

---

[1] James J. Gibson, *The Ecological Approach to Visual Perception* (Hillsdale, NJ: Lawrence Erlbaum, 1979).

tion this way: "Living cells... use DNA to construct the organism, not vice versa."[2] Many kinds of conjunctions and symbioses now appear to have significance for bio-history; these are evolutionary events that depend neither on natural selection nor mutation. The study of multi-cellularity shows that individuation and aggregation are both fundamental to living process, and are interdependent rather than mutually exclusive processes. Focus on the actions of cells has restored the importance of the life experience of the organism and its forms of relationality to evolutionary theory; bio-history is now seen to be created by mutually constitutive interactions between the genotype, the phenotype, and environmental, including social, affordances. The organism is no longer a "dead end," and evolution turns out to be a history of ecologies rather than of anthropomorphized "selfish" genes bent on self-replication. Semiosis—communication—is a sine qua non of living process. The brain's capacity for estimation and signal-interpretation is, simply, vital; only in very specific knowledge-ecologies does it require probability theory and experimental controls to act on behalf of sentient experience. Living process—including artful, real-time, improvisational activity—finally plays a significant role in bio-historiography.

Many forms of life enjoy meaning-making and interpreting; what Panksepp calls "SEEKING" is not, as some of our latter-day theorists would have it, a contemptible pleasure, but an aspect of living process.[3] By "communication," moreover, we do not intend simply "information-processing" or "de/coding of lexical messages." We honor the joy of utterance, the intersubjectivity it sponsors, and the affective-paraverbal features of language. As Bachelard once put it, "[b]eautiful words are already remedies."[4] It is, of course, important that we do not idealize the interconnectedness of living (as well as non-living)

---

[2] Jesper Hoffmeyer, *Biosemiotics: An Examination into the Signs of Life and the Life of Signs* (Chicago: University of Chicago Press, 2009), 32.

[3] Jaak Panksepp, *Affective Neuroscience: The Foundations of Human and Animal Emotions* (New York: Oxford University Press, 1998), 24–27, 51.

[4] Gaston Bachelard, *The Poetics of Reverie: Childhood, Language and the Cosmos*, trans. Daniel Russell (Boston: Beacon Press, 1969), 31.

matter, or assume that discourses thereof cannot be appropriated by powers inimical to creaturely enjoyment, like neoliberalism. But we can say that it is not possible to prosper all alone. Epidemiological studies show that poor health in the poorer ranks of a population predicts poorer health in its richer ranks as well. To speak of thriving, we know that lab rats grow bigger and stronger when their environments are "enriched"—that is to say, when they have lots of toys, meaningful activities, and opportunities to be curious and sociable. It is the same for us. As the evolutionary scientist J.Z. Young points out,[5] art matters to life; organisms want to live only when life is worth living. The Darwinist A.R. Wallace wrote in 1891 that "the popular idea of the struggle for existence entailing misery and pain on the animal world is the very reverse of the truth." What it seeks, and often finds, is the "maximum of life and of the enjoyment of life."[6]

Too many humanists think of science scientistically, and accept, and even idealize, its epistemological privilege, arguing, for example, that we should be doing science, or something that looks like it. We should take field observation as a model of descriptive reserve, when (ironically) *explication de texte* is currently being recommended as an important analytical method in the social sciences. We should also jettison *explication de texte*—as many literary historians have argued at least since the 1970s—in favor of watermark studies or the computation of geographical distribution of literary genres. Digital humanists have long insisted that if the humanities are to become competitive again, we must valorize and practice what amounts to engineering. By now, some of the results are in, and they are not impressive. In the English Department at the University of California, Santa Barbara, at least, where the digital humanities have been fostered (and rightly so) for two decades, the embrace thereof has not prevented the loss of office staff, significant FTE attrition, retention failure, and the like. We are told we must compete, but rhetoric about survival and competition belongs to an outdated understanding of evolution; the study of cooperation and

---

[5] J.Z. Young, *An Introduction to the Study of Man* (Oxford: Clarendon, 1971).
[6] A.R. Wallace, *Darwinism: A Exposition of the Theory of Natural Selection* (London: Macmillan, 1891), 40 (http://www.gutenberg.org/files/14558/14558-h/14558-h.htm).

mutual aid is now among the most vigorous sub-fields in evolutionary psychology and biology. Contemporary practitioners of the biological sciences were trained during the heydays of poststructuralism, multiculturalism and environmental theory; recall that Gibson's seminal work on affordances and the commingling of pro- and exteroception dates from the late 1970s. It is now de rigeur to recognize that, in work with human subjects, "human" does not mean "white middle class North American" graduate students; comparative psychology has gained enormously in importance since the days when scientists scorned multiculturalism as an attack on universals.

We hope that our interdisciplinary work will draw as much as possible, not on the exploded scientism of the past, but on the contemporary embrace of causal parity, plasticity, and real-time experimental ecologies. The humanities teach the arts of living—how to see, interpret, express, hear, and feel as richly and widely as possible. And they teach us how to practice those arts in the context of real-time, improvisational activity—the kind of thing we do every day, all day long, the significance of which must be restored as against the habituation that tempts us to take them for granted.

EPICUREAN RAIN

Speaking of habituation, this is how Isabelle Stengers describes what *she* does as a university researcher:

> One way of articulating what I do is that my work is not addressed to my colleagues. This is not about contempt, but about learning to situate oneself in relation to a future—a future in which I am uncertain as to what will have become of universities. . . . Defending them against external attacks (rankings, objective evaluation in all domains, the economy of knowledge) is not particularly compelling because of the passivity with which academics give in. This shows that it's over. Obviously, the interesting question is: who is going to take over? At the end of the era of the medieval university, it was not clear who would take over.[7]

---

[7] "The Care of the Possible: Isabelle Stengers Interviewed by Erik

It was not clear. Things are not clear, or they are very clear. It ain't over 'till it's over, or it's already over. We've entered an era of loving our catastrophes, of tuning them for scholarly fugues about the end of everything, where it's no longer about preparing for the end or even surviving that end, but about living on the rising waves and pandemic fumes of its temporal drag, where we cultivate and adorn shipwrecks instead of gardens.[8]

Speaking of drag, history's a real drag. It makes thinking hard, because you can't get out of it. It's always giving you headaches, especially if you work in a university of a certain Western-white-Anglo-German variety, which is almost all of them. There's no remedy for this, no over-the-library-counter medication. There are a lot of alternative histories but we call those "minor," they're at the "bottom," and there's never an alternative no-history. No blank pages. No Lucretian laminar void. The only thing to do in a laminar void is fall and bump into things, and that makes it the perfect setting for novelty and new relationalities—in fact, for history. History without laminar voids is not history; it's propaganda. Cruising is historical, or vice versa; we're speaking also of Bersani's "non-masochistic *jouissance* (one that owes nothing to the death drive)."[9] It means we *might* get to have our *jouissance* without demands, without insisting that someone else pay a price for it. And maybe also without always over-thinking it. Because history is a drag.

That's the tragedy of Meryl Streep as Susan Orlean in Charlie Kaufman's *Adaptation*, standing up to her waist in the Everglades swamp after her lover, the orchid thief John LaRoche, is eaten by a crocodile:

> Oh my God. Everything's over. I did everything wrong. I want my life back. I want it back before it got all fucked up. Let me be a baby again. I want to be new. I want to be new.

That's our tragedy, too.

Bordeleau," trans. Kelly Ladd, *Scapegoat* 1 (2011): 12 [12–27].
[8] Steve Mentz, *At the Bottom of Shakespeare's Ocean* (London: Continuum, 2009), 98.
[9] Leo Bersani, "Sociability and Cruising," in *Is the Rectum a Grave? And Other Essays* (Chicago: University of Chicago Press, 2010), 61 [45–62].

Becoming-new (as opposed to, say, Deleuze and Guattari's becoming-intense, becoming-animal, becoming-imperceptible, etc.[10]) feels practically impossible. We'll admit that we can't escape history, exactly, and that Epicurus's laminar void—through which atomic particles once "rained," and then, through various small "swerves" (Luctretius's *clinamen*),[11] created our world—is no longer possible (at least, not from the standpoint of the universe being empty). At the same time, we need not only to be able to account for novelty (isn't that partly what critical studies of art, for example, are about? and also historical studies?), but to also be able to create it, and this can't be accomplished without somehow charting returns to (or reboots of) that laminar void, in order to cultivate its radical contingency, its powers for engendering material encounters that can't be predicted in advance, and out of which alternative life- and art-practices become possible.

Why does novelty matter? Because without it, everything is always set to repeat, even with overtly subversive variations—Judith Butler's thinking on drag as performative repetition "with a difference," for example, where creative innovation is of course possible, but also always depends on iterations of the same and thus never entirely breaks free of its object of critique.[12] As Aaron Bady has argued recently, with regard to the institutional unrest within the University of California, critique "is often not very good at breaking away from its object; critique is dependent on its objects, and its objects will define the meaning and possibilities of critique." Further, to critique "can be to obey: by applying only where obedience is not required, this kind of free speech is just the flip side of power, a kind of supplementary and enabling excess."[13]

---

[10] See Gilles Deleuze and Félix Guattari, "1730: Becoming-Intense, Becoming-Animal, Becoming-Imperceptible . . . ," in *A Thousand Plateaus: Capitalism and Schizophrenia*, trans. Brian Massumi (Minneapolis: University of Minnesota Press, 1987).

[11] See David J. Furley, *Two Studies in the Greek Atomists* (Princeton: Princeton University Press, 1967), and Lucretius, *De Rerum Natura*, ed. Cyril Bailey, 3 vols. (Oxford: Oxford University Press, 1947).

[12] See Judith Butler, "Gender Is Burning: Questions of Appropriation and Subversion," in Judith Butler, *Bodies That Matter: On the Discursive Limits of "Sex"* (New York: Routledge, 1993), 121–140.

[13] Aaron Bady, "Bartleby in the University of California: The Social Life of Disobedience," *The New Inquiry: Zunguzungu* [weblog],

But this is just a caution, for we will always need critique (Bady himself never stops critiquing[14]) and it has not, contra Latour, "run out of steam." As long as there exist asymmetrical power relations and the capitalist-neo-liberal uptake-reification of everything, we will need critique, especially if, by "critique," we mean speaking truth to power, from within its relations, in order to insist that power account for itself, that it be held accountable (which is also a way of putting particular checks on power, from a position of "equal standing" and in full view of some sort of "commons"—at least, that's the optimistic view[15]). But we have to be able to envision a possibility of change, for the university, that might mean a new university that would betray its own history, one that might even arrive from what Althusser termed "the assignable nothingness of all swerve," situated in a no-place of aleatory encounter that Althusser imagined as being (if somewhat paradoxically) before history:

> In this 'world' without being or history (like Rousseau's forest), what happens? . . . What happens there is what happens in Epicurus's universal rain, prior to any world, any being and any reason as well as any cause. What happens is that there are encounters . . . . it is enough to know that it comes about 'we know not where, we do not know when,' and that it is the 'smallest deviation possible,' that is, the assignable nothingness of all swerve.[16]

Towards the end of his life, in the early 1980s, recently discharged from a psychiatric hospital in Paris, where he was hospitalized for three years after murdering his wife in

---

May 3, 2013: http://thenewinquiry.com/blogs/zunguzungu/bartleby-in-the-university-of-california-the-social-life-of-disobedience/.

[14] Witnessed, for example, by Bady's own stream of critical postings on his blog *zunguzungu* at *The New Inquiry*: http://thenewinquiry.com/blogs/zunguzungu/.

[15] On this point, see Michel Foucault on parrhesia in *Fearless Speech*, ed. Joseph Pearson (Los Angeles: Semiotext(e), 2001).

[16] Louis Althusser, "The Underground Current of the Materialism of the Encounter," in Louis Althusser, *Philosophy of the Encounter: Later Writings, 1978-1987*, eds. Oliver Corpet and François Matheron, trans. G.M. Goshgarian (London: Verso, 2006), 191 [163–207]. All subsequent quotations of this work cited parenthetically, by page number.

1980, and living in a neighborhood apart from the École normale supérieure that had formerly provided a more socially sheltered existence (and thus, working more in the Outside), Althusser threw himself into a work never to be completed on the "materialism of the encounter," which began simply, "It is raining. Let this book therefore be, before all else, a book about ordinary rain" (167). In this work, Althusser hoped to show that the most radical (and importantly, for him, anti-logocentric, anti-Meaning) philosophy of all would be one that takes account of the aleatory and the contingent as opposed to "necessity and teleology, that is to say, a . . . disguised form of idealism" (168).[17] Philosophy, for Althusser, would then become a practice of observation and description of "crystallized" encounters, out of which the world would "open up" to us, as a sort of "gift," "in the facticity of its contingency" (170). Philosophy would also dispense with the "problem" approach (i.e., "why is there something rather than nothing?") by "refusing to assign itself any 'object' whatsoever . . . in order to set out from nothing, and from the infinitesimal, aleatory variation of nothing constituted by the swerve of the fall" (174–175).

This is not to say that one avoids history—after all, the world is filled with millions of somethings, as opposed to black voids, and history "gels at certain felicitous moments" (194)—for example, Althusser's murder of his wife, which can never be undone[18]—but rather, in order for

---

[17] But it should also be noted here that a logocentric critique isn't—or in our view, shouldn't be—scorn for creaturely attachment to meaning-making as creative activity and meanings as creative productions. These are life-saving activities, after all, and key to thriving in this world.

[18] In a prologue to this unfinished book on "the materialism of the encounter," Althusser wrote, "in November 1980, in the course of a severe, unforeseeable crisis that had left me in a state of mental confusion, I strangled my wife, the woman who was everything in the world to me and who loved me so much that, since living had become impossible for her, she wanted only to die. In my confusion, not knowing what I was doing, I no doubt rendered her this 'service': she did not defend herself against it, but died of it" (164). This strange and quasi-emotionally distant "confession" (if it can be called such) is somehow more honest than the official confession Althusser wrote later in 1985, where he claimed he was only giving his wife a neck massage that somehow went awry and which induced in him a sort of hysterical amnesia (see Louis Al-

anything different to happen (and that is an ethical project, we would argue), one has to figure out strategies for creating special starting conditions that "void" (or at least temporarily "stay") presupposed parameters of thought and movement and allow one to attend to the shock and materialism of the encounter. There would never be any "final" conclusions or certainties, just a Rousseauvian forest in which "the radical absence of society . . . constitutes the essence of any possible society" (184). Ultimately, for Althusser, the materialism of the encounter "is the materialism, not of a subject (be it God or the proletariat), but of a process, a process that has no subject, yet imposes on the subjects (individuals or others) which it dominates the order of its development, with no assignable end" (190). All possible arrangements and complementarities possess a certain "readiness" for possibility, in such a world of collision (190, 192), and Meaning (with a capital "M") is no longer about origins or ends, but inheres instead in the felicity of encounter.

Let us work, then, to build a Rousseauvian forest, or Kaufmanesque swamp, in which we can practice our tiniest deviations. We need, of course, our "arts of living," which have a history (that we need not neglect) and which the traditional humanities has been so adept at cultivating, but this also means that the humanities is a reservoir of the sorts of creative delusions (and fuzzy thinking) that are necessary for not just surviving, but thriving. As the poet Lisa Robertson has written, "I need to be able to delude myself, for as long as it takes, as long as it takes to translate an emotion, a grievance, a politics, an intoxication, to a site, an outside."[19] We need our delusional spaces. The University, and the humanities especially, is a space, as we've stated above, for the artfulness of living, for enriched environments, and real-time experimental ecologies—which is to say, for alternate delusions, and this means we

---

thusser, *The Future Lasts Forever: A Memoir* [New York: New Press, 1995]). We mention these biographical details because, in reading Althusser's late writing on a "materialism of the encounter," one can't help but feel that his search for a philosophy of the radically empty, of the contingent encounter from which anything was possible, was also somehow a search for his own void from which to begin, again.

[19] Lisa Robertson, "The Weather: A Report on Sincerity," *DC Poetry* (2001): http://www.dcpoetry.com/anthology/242.

also need an alternate delusion for the University.[20] We've never liked the phrase, "what's Plan B?" But honestly, what *is* Plan B?

Who will take over? You know what's missing in Isabelle Stengers's comment—"At the end of the era of the medieval university, it was not clear who would take over"? The what. Who's going to take over *what*? The "diplomatic institution" called a university, which is already dead, or maybe just a little ruined? A little ruination never hurt anyone. This world looks beautiful in the light of a ruined moon, in the dusk of the carbon dust of a ruined world. But it might look better in the hail of an Epicurean rain. And you know what that means? We need to go outside, where it's raining.

Who's going to take over what? How about if, when they get here, there's nothing to take over? Because we dispersed, and went rogue-medieval-itinerant? We went out in the rain. We might decide, with Michael O'Rourke, to seek out "a recalibrated futurity for the humanities which recognizes that its future will always have been its end, which, more affirmatively put, is to say that its future will have been always to begin its ending again. . . . [and] we can find a certain dignity in what we are doing if we maintain absolute fidelity to the incalculable and unreckonable event of the university to-come, the university without condition."[21] This will also mean embracing what Geoffrey Bennington has written, by way of Derrida, about

---

[20] On the subject of the ways in which the university, and especially the humanities, have been undermined and how they might reclaim new space(s) among the "ruins," as it were, see (among other works), L.O. Aranye Fradenburg, *Staying Alive: A Survival Manual for the Liberal Arts* (Brooklyn: punctum books, 2013), and Bill Readings, *The University in Ruins* (Cambridge, MA: Harvard University Press, 1997). On how the university has reached its current state of troubling affairs, see Christopher Newfield, *Unmaking the Public University: The Forty-Year Assault on the Middle Class* (Cambridge, MA: Harvard University Press, 2008), and Benjamin Ginsberg, *The Fall of the Faculty: The Rise of the All-Administrative University and Why It Matters* (Oxford, UK: Oxford University Press, 2011).

[21] Michael O'Rourke, "After," *In The Middle*, November 29, 2010: http://www.inthemedievalmiddle.com/2010/11/guest-post-michael-orourke-after.html. This post is a transcript of O'Rourke's keynote address at the 1st biennial meeting of the BABEL Working Group held in Austin, Texas in November 2010.

the institutionality of the university:

> The University . . . [has] a responsibility to foster events of thought that cannot fail to unsettle the University in its Idea of itself. . . . On this account, the University is in principle the institution that 'lives' the precarious chance and ruin of the institution as its very institutionality.[22]

So let's affirm some ruinous possibility now—that means knowing your history, but also when to let go of it, and to be willing to remain perpetually unsettled, both in terms of knowledge disciplines, but also in terms of place, or as Simone Weil once put it, "we must take the feeling of being at home into exile. We must be rooted in the absence of place."[23] The university isn't only a place, it's also a state of mind. Wherever we are, wherever we gather, wherever we profess—that is the university, and there will never be a take-over of that situation.

But we have to get out in the rain and also learn how to make it rain. We have to go outside and join hands with the ever-growing academic labor precariat and start forming new initiatives for para-academic outstitutions.[24] It's a question of the atmosphere, and how we need to be more drenched in it. And as Derrida wrote, "take your time, but be quick about it, because you do not know what awaits you."[25]

---

[22] Geoffrey Bennington, "Foundations," *Textual Practice* 21.2 (2007): 231–249.

[23] Simone Weil, *Gravity and Grace*, ed. Gustave Thibon (London: Routledge & Kegan Paul, 1952), 86.

[24] Here we are making a nod toward new educational (and occasionally anti-institutional) and alt-cult initiatives and start-ups, such as the Brooklyn Institute for Social Research (http://thebrooklyninstitute.com/), The Public School New York (http://thepublicschool.org/nyc), *continent.* journal (http://www.continentcontinent.com/index.php/continent), punctum books (http://punctumbooks.com), and The Bruce High Quality Foundation (http://www.thebrucehighqualityfoundation.com/), just to name a few. We borrow the term "outstitution" from Paul Boshears.

[25] Jacques Derrida, "The Future of the Profession or the University Without Condition (thanks to the 'Humanities," what could take place tomorrow)," in *Jacques Derrida and the Humanities: A Critical Reader*, ed. Tom Cohen (Cambridge, UK: Cambridge University Press, 2001), 24–57.

Time Change/
Mode Change

Allan Mitchell and Will Stockton

The circle drawn, the authors step inside, seeking safety from the spirits. They are skeptical about this whole conjuration business, however, and fearful, too, of the boredom that comes with not being possessed. So they tarry over their books.

AM: "Settle thy studies, Faustus, and begin / To sound the depths of that thou wilt profess."[1] Thinking about what to do next we are liable to be haunted by past efforts, perhaps by a diabolical presence such as this German *magus*, mocking any attempts to enumerate all we've tried and to propose some new and occult mode of inquiry. As if suc-

---

[1] Christopher Marlowe, *Dr. Faustus*, ed. Roma Gill (New York: W.W. Norton & Co., 1989), 1.1–2.

cessive attempts to do more, or better, with less would be sufficiently original ("Foucault farewell! Where is Harman?"). Should we always be in pursuit of The Next Big Thing? Perhaps the first thing to consider is the risk that in seeking to gain divinity, we will lack all ambition to invent other futures. "Lines, circles, schemes, letters, and characters! / Ay, these are those that Faustus most desires. O what a world of profit and delight, / Of power, of honour, of omnipotence / Is promised the studious artisan!"[2] But is that what we really want now?

WS [*furrowing his brow*]: You asked if I wanted to conjure devils. Now it seems you really brought me out here to talk about the future of the humanities. [*WS puts down the book he is reading, Amanda Cross's* Death in a Tenured Position.]

Let's at least be clear about etymology if we're going to worry about the future, however wicked. There's no way to be original, to pursue "Things unattempted yet in Prose or Rhyme," without returning to origins.[3] The future of the humanities must be ancient. As we try to conjure new devils, then, let's not banish the old ones; they are our friends. It's those lines, circles, schemes, letters and characters we use to conjure them that have created mundane obstacles, so-called greater practical tasks, standing like a wide STEM in the way of a new future. Let's not hesitate to incant old names.

[*AM starts rifling through the bag of books.*]

WS: See if you can find my dearest Milton in there. No stranger to demons and known to party with Satan, Milton thought that future of the human—of the humanities—looked bleak, which is why he sat down and wrote poems.

AM [*still rummaging and stopping to admire another volume*]: Long before Milton, you know, the humanities were considered, in more than one sense, *trivial*. I know we tend to speak of the *modern* corporate university, but even in his day John of Salisbury defended the humanities against contemporary entrepreneurial types who rejected

---

[2] Marlowe, *Dr. Faustus*, 1.51–55.
[3] John Milton, *Paradise Lost*, in *Complete Poems and Major Prose*, ed. Merritt Y. Hughes (Indianapolis: Bobbs-Merrill, 1957), 1.16.

the arts in favor of professional training that would produce personal wealth.[4] I fear there has always been a "crisis" in the humanities, that an originary *krisis* is somehow inherent to them; the sooner we accept our critical condition, the better. What we are doing is at least always emergent and at a decision point. Yes, yes, let the future be ancient. Shakespeare was wrong, I think. The past is not prologue; the past is an invention that calls for new creations.

WS: We must talk some time about your assumption that Shakespeare possesses Prospero's voice. But later. John of Salisbury, Shakespeare, Milton do take us back, [*WS becomes distracted by other memories.*] If only *Back to the Future* were about a mad poet instead of a mad scientist! I think that movie actually introduced me to time travel—to thinking about history as something other than a straightforward, irreversible line. [*WS begins to trace the outline of the USS Enterprise NCC 1701-A on the ground.*] I usually give *Star Trek: The Next Generation* the credit, what with its late twentieth-century view of the twenty-fourth century. But really I forget where I first learned to think about the possibilities and types of time travel. And about forgetting as one mode of time travel—one central to the humanities, as Milton himself shows us in a poem driven at once by his inability to remember a time before and his determination to invent it through art.

AM: Your darling Milton and Shakespeare! How immodest, after all, was Milton's rejection of the "middle flight" of those who demand less of literary studies, his determination "to soar / Above th' *Aonian* Mount"?[5] One might almost be forgiven for thinking Milton had forgotten himself, daring to fly above the abode of the muses. He could hardly avoid the fates of Icarus and Phaeton—or of Satan. Aim that high and you end up in the nether regions!

[*AM pauses, reconsiders.*]

But, to be fair, Milton understood the perils well, and so knowingly recollects Dante, Boccaccio, Ariosto, who al-

---

[4] John of Salisbury, *The Metalogicon: A Twelfth-Century Defense of the Verbal and Logical Arts of The Trivium*, trans. Daniel D. McGarry (Philadelphia: Paul Dry, 2009), 19–20.
[5] Milton, *Paradise Lost*, 1.14–15.

ready promised "things unattempted."[6] The poet's bold, modernizing move is at once an epic medievalism, and situates text and reader within a postlapsarian genealogy. His boundless satanic ambitions help redraw the original dilemma for the humanities, in some weird way. His verses express other measures, quite apart from reigning administrative metrics and progress narratives. But what apparition is this?

> [*Music sounds, and the ghost of the poet passes over the stage*]

WS: Tiresias reincarnate! How did we manage this conjuration? By what art? [*Exeunt the ghost.*] And where is he going? Back to his father's house—again, as after university—because he isn't through reading? [*WS falls to his knees, extends his hands upward.*] Oh honor the ghost who reminds us to honor forgetting! To keep reading! [*WS's hands fall. He has remembered something.*] That reminds me: have we forgotten how we learned to read? John Locke forgot, and argued that children learning to read must be tricked: play a dice-game, he suggests, in which each face bears a letter. When the game is long forgotten, the knowledge of letters will remain. Rousseau mocks Locke's idea, and teaches Émile to read by writing him a note containing details of an outing; Emile will not be able to attend the outing unless he can make sense of what it says. But Rousseau confesses that he too has forgotten how he learned to read. Furthermore, Locke and Rousseau say these things in books I've forgotten I've read![7] How then do those of us who teach reading—whether at basic or more advanced, critical levels—quantify, measure, and value forgetting? How much time does one need to forget

---

[6] On the commonplace, see Ernst Robert Curtius, *European Literature and the Latin Middle Ages* (Princeton: Princeton University Press, 1983), 86–87.

[7] WS read both books in college, but remembers he read them only when reading his colleague Brian McGrath's book *The Poetics of Unremembered Acts: Reading, Lyric, Pedagogy* (Evanston: Northwestern University Press, 2013), 6–8. For the originals, see John Locke, *Some Thoughts Concerning Education* and *Of the Conduct of the Understanding*, eds. Ruth W. Grant and Nathan Tarcov (Indianapolis: Hackett, 1996), 114, and Jean-Jacques Roussaeu, *Émile, or On Education*, trans. Allan Bloom (New York: Basic Books, 1979), 117.

before one realizes what one learns? How do we defend forgetting as fundamental to the experience of a humanities education?

AM [*tossing Milton forgetfully back in the bag, digging now for Chaucer*]: I am tempted to state within this circle, in this *séance,* that it is by forgetting ourselves in study that we are educated: *educare*, drawn or led out into other spaces and times, to strange new lives and new worlds. Language acquisition requires a sort of becoming-oblivious in order to be literate, orienting ourselves, by means of so many material supports, to regard others outside. And yet there is a lot to remember to properly lose oneself in the best possible way—an *inventory* is a condition of *invention*, someone said before. [*He opens a book to read aloud*]: "For out of olde feldes, as men seyth, / Cometh al this newe corn yer to yere, / And out of olde bokes, in good feyth, / Cometh al this newe science that men lere."[8] Here we return to the original notion of what we owe to old books. Yet someone must still work the field, from whence comes this "newe corn yer to yere," which is what I dream our students are doing in essays, and exams and we engage in here. It is also, in another and less transactional mode, what makes learning so contingent.

WS: I agree, but given the prevailing administrative metrics, we humanities scholars are never really allowed to *forget* what we're doing, and are scarcely permitted to say, when asked why we exist or what we're producing, that we don't know, or that we're comfortable not knowing. The pedagogical question then becomes how best to plan and make space for all of these zombie-like creatures, these specters of Milton, Rousseau, Chaucer, even ourselves. The future of the humanities sits in our classrooms, but most students don't understand their conjuring powers. [*The opening lines of Whitney Houston's* "The Greatest Love of All" *sound in WS's head. The spirit of Lee Edelman retaliates with a deliberately off-key rendition of* "Tomorrow."] Most of us bemoan this ignorance, which is not necessarily their fault, and try to correct for it by building an elaborate scaffold of learning outcomes on our syllabi.

---

[8] Geoffrey Chaucer, *Parliament of Fowls*, in *The Riverside Chaucer*, ed. Larry D. Benson, 3rd edn. (Boston: Houghton Mifflin, 1987), 22–25.

But what if, instead, we harness this ignorance to the obliviousness necessary for literacy. An immodest, utopian proposal from within the safety of this circle: let us delete all course objectives from our syllabi—all things that seek in advance to tell the student what he or she will learn. The course title alone should suffice for the preview. If students ask what they will learn, reply that you do not know (because you don't). If students seek a model for *how* they should learn, point them to *Othello*, a play about reading, only remove Act V so they don't think your course will end tragically.

AM: Nor would it end tragically if Othello were a better reader, less violently certain of himself—perhaps, too, less susceptible to the devastating effects of his own racist, misogynistic imagination. The humanities should be a place for safe stumbling, a place to forget what we're doing and to figure it out later; it should encouraged people to try on ideas that do not have a secure place in the world, or not yet. The humanities need a new kind of modal logic: *necessarily, everything is contingent*. And history needs new modes of transit, including long forgotten forms of transport, such as sojourning, wandering, veering, as we drift towards futures with which we are not yet affiliated.

WS [*rifles through the pile of books they have now created*]: First things first, though. Because we put together this syllabus that I'm guessing will simply say—"In this class, seek to soar above the Aonian mount. You must be comfortable with devils. Gardening experience desired but not required"—we're going to need new texts. These are all marked up and torn. How do you even read them? They're so old.

AM: But that's the point! We are often unaware of what is archaic or contemporary anyway; the past is infinitely ramified in the present and future. Thinking about things simply as old does not capture this overlap. We need new metaphors. Where's my copy of the conversation with Michel Serres? [*WS hands it to him.*] Here: "Consider a late-model car. It is a disparate aggregate of scientific and technical solutions dating from different periods. One can date it component by component: this part was invented at the turn of the century, another, ten years ago . . . . Not to mention that the wheel dates back to Neolithic times."[9] I propose that we are more likely to get where we want, whether in our scholarship or in class, if we think of time as less a linear than a stochastic system—the "folded or crumpled time" in which we are all implicated.

Serres offers another apt metaphor for this time; in fact, one you will like more—the crumpled handkerchief. "Two distant points suddenly are close, even superimposed," which were separated by distances when the handkerchief was set out flat.[10] Pleated or torn, fixed points on a planar surface exhibit a new rapport. Folding up a map might produce a superior model for us to follow into the future.

WS: I see what you did there, you sly devil. For Othello, who fails miserably to read the handkerchief, can only conceive of the future as a "chaos" if he loses his present anchor, Desdemona.[11] Othello can't forget, like he needs to, the racist superstructure of his past and imagine a new future for himself and Desdemona.[12] Poor illiterate *demon* Ot*hell*o.

I think that if there's a *sentence* amidst all this *solas*, it's that we as humanities scholars cannot defer the future— imagining it as something we want but which we do not enact. If we are to break out of this mode that brings us again and again to the point of talking about what we *would* do, we have to imagine the future and bring it with us. We have to do what we are doing right here, right now.

AM [*going meta*]: In this circle? By means of this cento-like assemblage? I should say so. For what are we doing in this ensorcelled moment but stitching times and modes together? Creating another patchworked text. A scaffold for future being. There is much to remember in order to forget ourselves, doing what we do here, right now.

---

[9] Michel Serres and Bruno Latour, *Conversations on Science, Culture, and Time*, trans. Roxanne Lapidus (Ann Arbor: The University of Michigan Press, 1995), 45.
[10] Serres and Latour, *Conversations on Science*, 60.
[11] William Shakespeare, *Othello*, ed. Russ McDonald (New York: Penguin, 2001), 3.3.92.
[12] WS remembers here Linda Charnes, "Shakespeare, and Belief, in the Future," in *Presentist Shakespeares*, ed. Hugh Gray and Terence Hawkes (New York: Routledge, 2007), 64–78.

WORLD CHANGE/
SEA CHANGE

Lowell Duckert and Steve Mentz

BIRD FUTURES

In the future I want, I am a cormorant. A screeching sea-crow, I perch on a high branch on the Tree of Life overlooking Paradise. My eyes flare with greed, and with two senses of the word "want." Things appear down there, spread out below me, things that I lack ("want") and things that I desire ("want").

"Various" is the word for what I see. "A happy rural seat of various view" (4.247) is the full line in *Paradise Lost*, but it's just "various" that I crave.[1] These three syllables roll around inside my bird's mouth. Various. All of the things that inhabit this Paradise, laid out before me. Not

---

[1] John Milton, *Paradise Lost*, ed. David Scott Kastan (Indianapolis: Hackett Publishing, 2005), 4.247. Satan sits "like a cormorant" at 4.196.

just one thing, but another.

COLD WAR OF THE WORLDS

The world change I imagine happens where the world is changing the fastest: the Arctic Circle. In September 2008, the MV *Camilla Desgagnés*, the first commercial ship to sail through the Northwest Passage, did so almost entirely unobstructed. At this current rate of climate change, scientists at UCLA predict an ice-free passage by mid-century.[2] Such an opening opens up a series of geopolitical problems: to whom do these shipping lanes belong? What of the resources yet to be discovered underneath the ice? The express mission of the Arctic Council, formed in 1996 and comprised of eight nations and several indigenous groups, is to preemptively tackle these issues—or else face another cold war.[3] I am reminded of another passage forged six years before the *Camilla*'s voyage: Bruno Latour's argument in *War of the Worlds: What about Peace?* "[W]hat is needed is a new recognition of the old wars we have been fighting all along—in order to bring about new kinds of negotiation, and a new kind of peace."[4] For Latour, it is better to be at war and to think about diplomacy than to imagine that there is no war at all and to hold fast to modernity's progress. One recognition of the old war occurred in the summer of 2012 when record amounts of Arctic sea ice melted. Cold comfort for world change. But what else can we learn from this war zone? Can peace ever be ensured? And are there new kinds of negotiation to be found in what is predicted to be one of the world's most *negotiable* passageways?

AVIAN TRUTHS

From my crow's mouth I scream three horrifying truths:

---

[2] Laurence C. Smith and Scott R. Stephenson, "New Trans-Arctic Shipping Routes Navigable by Midcentury," *Proceedings of the National Academy of Sciences Plus*, March 4, 2013; DOI: 10.1073/pnas.1214212110.

[3] Paul Arthur Berkman, "Preventing an Arctic Cold War," *The New York Times*, March 12 2013: http://www.nytimes.com/2013/03/13/opinion/preventing-an-arctic-cold-war.html.

[4] Bruno Latour, *War of the Worlds: What About Peace?* (Chicago: Prickly Paradigm Press, 2002), 4.

Truth #1: Change fractures our desire for wholeness. It will break, all of it.

Truth #2: A better name for this planet would be Ocean, not Earth.

Truth #3: Salt water tastes bitter, flavored with the recognition that nothing lasts.

These truths send me searching. Can I find passages through the sea ice?

My view from the Tree is wide and broad. In the tangled thickets, I find what I am looking for. I see Heteronyms.

The term "heteronym" refers to a member of a large group of imaginary personae, numbering over 70, in which the great 20th-century Portuguese poet Fernando Pessoa wrote. These authors, each of whom has an individual name, style, biography, and physical characteristics, collectively represent a rage for variety amid the poverty of identity. Multiple names and multiple selves become ways to navigate our over-abundant world, the too-many Paradises over which we look. Author-ness and its *auctoritee* become various, and the original self appears one of many voices, and not the most important one. The most influential heteronym, Alberto Caeiro, also overlooks Paradise when he writes poems. "I don't pretend to be anything more than the greatest poet in the world," Cairo claims. "I made the greatest discovery worth making, next to which all other discoveries are games of stupid children. I noticed the Universe."[5] Noticing is what I do, too, on this high branch. Seeing things in their differences and variety.

My question for the future is: how can we become heteronyms? Through what not-yet-opened passage must we pass? My future does not yet break open icy seas, but sits here, high on my branch, peering out at the world's change. Variously.

---

[5] Fernando Pessoa, *A Little Larger than the Entire Universe: Selected Poems*, ed. and trans. Richard Zenith (New York: Penguin, 2006), 6. This quotation appears in Zenith's introduction.

Ring Them Bells

Return again to the sea change happening at the top of the world, for here you might find different Arctic counsel, here is advice about how to shape the humanities and the sciences simultaneously in a changing world. I am reminded of (yet) another passage, this one unfurled before us by Michel Serres: "[This new map] transports us, in fact, from one major body of knowledge to the opposite one through the North-West passage. In geography, the carillon of the hard sciences finally falls silent, when that of the human sciences is barely beginning. In this almost silent space lies the landscape."[6] For Serres, the Northwest Passage is less a physical location and more an interchange between the local and global, the geological and political, the human and exact sciences. In this heteroscape of wet and dry, geography actively transports; like ice that hardens, melts, and carves, nothing is constant here except fluctuation itself. Passages ceaselessly emerge; maps must continually be redrawn. The Northwest Passage offers a way to think about being *between* (like a solid and a liquid, like a poet and a scientist), about being endlessly connective. Let us not only ring the bells of alarm—iceberg, dead ahead!—but also strike up a carillon call of collaboration between disciplines, beings. Peals never quiet in the almost silent seascape.

Disquiet Waters

My crow's eyes snatch more quick glances down from the Tree of Life over icy vastness. I'm on the lookout for more heteronyms, and I find two.

The first glance finds Bernando Soares, technically a semi-heteronym because of his close resemblance to the biographical Pessoa, and *The Book of Disquiet* (*Livro de Desassossego*), his "factless autobiography." In a fragment that may or may not have been intended for the final work, he writes about human encounters with hostile oceans:

Shipwrecks? No, I never suffered any. But I have

---

[6] Michel Serres, *The Five Senses: A Philosophy of Mingled Bodies*, trans. Margaret Sankey and Peter Cowley (New York: Continuum, 2008), 274.

the impression that I shipwrecked all my voyages,
and that my salvation lay in interspaces of unconsciousness.[7]

The whirl of heteronyms teaches shipwreck as identity and "salvation," demonstrating that no voyage arrives without disaster. Therefore we embrace suffering and seek "interspaces." In the sprawling mass of *The Book of Disquiet*, Soares slogs through failure and anonymity toward the partial and difficult consolations of art. "I don't sleep," writes Soares. "I interexist."[8] From my perch in the Tree I want to go down to him, light on his shoulder, nibble on his ear. His interspaces and intermixing structures my future.

I also spy another salty one, my favorite, Álvaro de Campos, crying out from the wharf-side or water's edge, looking for passage or arriving after a long journey:

> Wharf blackly reflected in still waters
> The bustle on board ships,
> O wandering, restless soul of people who live in ships,
> Of symbolic people who come and go, and for whom nothing lasts,
> For when the ship returns to port
> There's always some change on board![9]

Campos sings what the sea lures us into accepting. Even music won't hold us in place. There is no stillness in the future I want.

And now I hear him cry out again, he who wants what I also want, who craves what I crave—

> To have the audacity of sailcloth in the wind!
> To be, like the topsails, the whistling of the winds!
> An old guitar playing a fado about seas rife with dangers,
> A song for sailors to hear and not repeat![10]

---

[7] Fernando Pessoa, "A Voyage I Never Made (III)," in Fernando Pessoa, *The Book of Disquiet*, ed. and trans. Richard Zenith (New York: Penguin, 2001), 463.
[8] Pessoa, *The Book of Disquiet*, 242.
[9] Pessoa, "Maritime Ode," in *A Little Larger Than the Entire Universe*, 168.
[10] Pessoa, "Maritime Ode," in *A Little Larger Than the Entire Universe*, 178.

The music helps, even as it vanishes. Campos's ecstatic lines burrow into the variety of this visible Paradise, moving from sharing "audacity" with rippling sailcloth to becoming that same cloth "whistling" in the winds, to nestling finally inside an old guitar's dreams. For an instant, in the poem's no-time, bodies slough away and self is nothing more than sound. With no repeating when we're done singing.

THIRD COAST

Before the mid-morning panel at which the first instantiation of this joint future was performed, we drove fifty miles West from Kalamazoo to the shore of Lake Michigan for an icy immersion. The intensity of that experience echoed in the presentation and continues to vibrate. Here, at the center of our shared future, is what it felt like—

> When you dive into cold water, it pushes the wind out of you. The icy shock holds you still, just for an instant. You slide beneath the waves into water's slippery grip, and then lurch back up onto unsteady feet. Now everything's different. The air bites exposed skin, but it isn't just the cold or even the wind raking the lake into ragged swells. Something else. Your breath comes in near-frantic wrenches, and you can nearly feel some hidden motions inside your body, some awakened fire, constricted now inside loose ropes of cold. The lakewater has encircled your body, taken you whole—that's what immersion means—but after you stand up it gradually sloughs itself away. Second by second your breathing reasserts its rhythm. You plunge under a second time, and the cold comes back, but nothing like the first shock.
>
> The shock of immersion becomes the shock of emersion. When you dip into the Great Lake, you realize that the cold does not sedate your senses; it propels you to compose, to make passage to a lecture hall, to present the future you want, the future with the water you were within that morning and that you still carry on your skin. The dip is an emergence that signals a *mergence*—a watery interchange between human and nonhuman, an ice-

cold interspace inherent in Lake Michigan's very name: a Chippewa Indian word, *meicigama*, "great water," an overflowing vastness that the earliest colonizers could not comprehend, only absorb into their language. To these early swimmers, this place, like the newfound geopolitical Arctic of today, must have had its share of councils. What negotiations were made? What wars? What peace? You imagine the figures that have passed through, like you, the littoral zone of the lake, this inland sea. Heteronymous convoys. Conveyances.

MARY MAGDALENE

Crows are voracious. I spy another glittering one, this time a saint with many names and identities, a medieval precursor to Pessoa's plural auto-piracy of selves. She swims in the icy waters with us. This is how Jacobus de Voragine begins her story in *The Golden Legend*:

> The name Mary, or Maria, is interpreted as amarum mare, bitter sea, or as illuminator or illuminated. These three meanings are accepted as stranding for three shares or parts, of which Mary made the best choices, namely, the part of penance, the part of inward contemplation, and the part of heavenly glory.[11]

It's the "or" that gets me, Miltonic devil-bird that I am. The sudden shift from bitter seas to illumination, or to illuminator: is the saint the means or the end? Or is it precisely her plurality that sanctifies, her shifting bitter salt-tasting light that shows and tells?

As the story continues the name proliferates:

> Mary is called Magdalene, which is understood to mean "remaining guilty," or it means armed, or unconquered, or magnificent. (1:375)

Again later:

---

[11] Jacobus de Voragine, *The Golden Legend*, trans. William Granger Ryan, 2 vols. (Princeton: Princeton University Press, 1995), 1:374. Further citations noted parenthetically in the text.

Mary's cognomen "Magdalene" comes from Magdalum, the name of one of her ancestral properties. (1:375)

So many stories attach to these names, from sin to cleansing to evangelical voyages without sails, God propelling our saint from the Holy Land to the south of France. Plays are written in a late-fifteenth century East Midlands dialect of Middle English.[12] Dan Brown gets in on the act.[13] The point is: change attracts. Everyone wants variety.

KARL BUSHBY

Figure 1. Karl Bushby on the Alaskan coast. Photo by Dimitri Kieffer.

---

[12] This manuscript play is part of Bodleian MS Digby 133. For a recent study, see Susan Carter, "The Digby *Mary Magdalene*: Constructing the *Apostola Apostolorum*," *Studies in Philology* 106.4 (2009): 402–419.

[13] Dan Brown's bestseller, *The Da Vinci Code* (New York: Doubleday, 2003), relies on conspiratorial fantasies about Mary Magdalene and Jesus widely circulated in Michael Baigent, Richard Leigh, and Henry Lincoln's *The Holy Blood and the Holy Grail* (London: Jonathan Cape, 1982).

"Passage" comes from the Latin *passus* meaning "pace," and the Northwest Passage asks us to keep up the pace with the changing world. Over two weeks in March 2006, the British pacemaker Karl Bushby walked almost sixty miles on ice across the Bering Land Bridge from Alaska to Russia: an impossible feat because the Bering Land Bridge no longer exists (Fig. 1); it disappeared over ten thousand years ago, we are told, buried under the Bering Strait.

Not for Bushby, however; the crossing is just one leg in his ongoing Goliath Expedition in which he is to walk with "an unbroken footpath" (meaning, unassisted by vehicles) nearly forty thousand miles from Chile to England.[14] He passed through an interstitial space of freeze and thaw to tell us that we do not need to bridge divides between two giant continents, like the humanities and the sciences, that sit opposed along their straits of demarcation. We are already passing through.

CUSTANCE

Does the cormorant want always to be a cormorant? Might this, too change? Can I find a singularity in the worldsea, a still point, anchoring me to some piece of Paradise? I want some peace in my future.

In Chaucer's "Man of Law's Tale" there is a woman who represents variety amid the paradox of the singular at sea. Alone like Bushby, she voyages into variety:

> And in a ship al steereless, God woot,
> They han hir set, and bidde hire lerne saille,
> Out of Surrye agaynward to Ytaille. (439–441)[15]

Later, after many travels, she returns home:

> "I am youre doghter Custance," quod she,
> "That whilom ye han sent unto Surrye.
> It am I, fader, that in the salte see
> Was put alone and dampned for to dye.
> Now, goode fader, mercy I yow crye!" (1107–1111)

---

[14] See the Goliath Expedition's website: http://www.odysseyxxi.com/.
[15] Geoffrey Chaucer, "The Man of Law's Tale," *The Riverside Chaucer*, gen. ed. Larry D. Benson, 3rd edn. (Boston: Houghton Mifflin, 1987). Citations given by line numbers in the text.

To be still the same after so much sea! "It am I," she tells her father. Still Custance after all these years. That's what the tale tells: some names survive at sea. Does her constancy invert heteronymity? Does she assert a constant *I* as a hedge against the too-much variety flowing all around her, its winds and currents? I don't think so. She's looking for passage, like all of us, and finds it, eventually, everywhere.

GUIDO VAN DER WERVE

Figure 2. Guido van der Werve, *Nummer acht, everything is going to be alright* (2007). Courtesy of the artist and Luhring Augustine, New York.

What change do I want from this passing interchange? Why, *peace*. So what about it? I suggest that we pass . . . and trespass. Bushby's passage also teaches us that even a mistaken divide remains *divisive* nonetheless. Russian authorities ultimately halted his pace, detaining him for entering the country at an unauthorized entry point (the latest update as of April 2012 is that the Russian government has denied him a visa). For them, the "pass" bordered too close to the "trespass" (literally "passing across"). Yet what if we thought of trespassing not as an act of passing across a series of predetermined (and policed) borders frozen in place, but a process that shows how these contingent borders are constantly being re/defined by beings, like Bushby, who are passing through? We begin to recognize *how* we do it—and thereby imagine new ways of negotiating future interactions. The choice to dip in or dip out of Arctic space (for example) is a false one; we are dipping, we are passing through, *always*. Consider the Dutch artist Guido van der Werve walking slowly in front of an icebreaker that pushes its way through Finland's Gulf of Bothnia (Fig. 2).[16]

Nummer Acht conveys the relationships between humans, technology, and ice that need to be renegotiated; nothing walks alone, unaided by the others. Even more significantly, "Acht" communicates an image of protest. What would it mean to walk in front of the multitude of commercial vessels as they plunge into the open/ing seas of the Northwest Passage, ships that might be the harbingers of cold war? To impede the "progress" of modernity, to trespass in the name of ethics, in the name of peace?

Walk on: the world change I propose here is not easy, and it certainly does not require a world without ice—or any "impediments" (anything which "shackles the feet") for that matter. We actually need impediments to pace: those things that attach to our feet like ice bridges underfoot, that give us freedom *because of* their bonds, and that direct our pace into new passages, into new maps of knowledge. (Ernest Shackleton was the world's greatest trespasser.) The future I want starts by rethinking the "trespass" not as the illegal endeavor it has come to be but as a "passage across" that is full of potential—for the humanities-sciences interchange, for the ecocritics who explore these interstices like pacing Bushbys and van der Werves, and for those of us who ponder ways to keep up the *pace*, to keep the *peace*, with a changing world.

SEA CHANGE AND/AS WORLD CHANGE

Can we sing it again, that old anthem? All together? The way we did at Kalamazoo:

Nothing of him that doth fade
But doth suffer a sea change

---

[16] Thanks to Karl Steel for directing us to this image.

Into something rich and strange?[17]

In our future we will sing it once more, and not repeat it.

In our future we will sing the carillon of the various, and pass it along disquietly.

---

[17] William Shakespeare, *The Tempest*, ed. Virginia Mason Vaughan and Alden T. Vaughan (London: Arden, 2011), 1.2.400–402.

Voice Change/ Language Change

Jonathan Hsy and Chris Piuma

Please note: This is a translation of a talk. It was originally intended to be performed aloud as a conference paper. It has been translated for the page. In this version, there will be twenty sections (not counting the figures and their captions). Each section will consist of one hundred words, making a total of two thousand words. Every hundred words, there will be a switch between writers: now Chris, but soon Jonathan. Each section will serve as a container, separated by a boundary marker and a change between italics and roman type. This will separate my voice from Jonathan's.

Languages are slippery, and they don't like being contained.

We have already broken the rules. That was not one hundred words. That was far, far less than one hundred words.

Each section, we agreed, should consist of one hundred words. That section could have easily been rewritten to consist of one hundred words. We have already broken the rules. But. But now I am reminding you all of the rules. And now, in this section, we are being mindful of the rules, the rules that we have created and that we are breaking. We are being mindful of how we are creating them and how we are breaking them.

Figures 1-2. Points of articulation. Isidore's *Etymologies* above and T-O map right; adapted from Jean Mansel, *La Fleur des Histoires* (Valenciennes, 1459-1463). Bruxelles, Bibliothèque Royale de Belgique, MS 9231, fol. 281v.

In his *Etymologies*, Isidore initially suggests each language [*lingua*] can be traced to one nation [*natio*], but he soon gives up on this idea, re-distributing all languages across different groups of people by stereotyped mode of utterance (IX.1). Oriental peoples [*Omnes ... Orientis gentis*], for instance, gurgle in the throat [*in gutture*], Mediterranean people [*Omnes mediterranae gentes*] crush the palate [*in palato*], Westerners [*Omnes Occidentis gentes*] gnash the teeth [*in dentibus*] (IX.8). These body parts seem to be evenly dispersed across space: Eastern throats, Mediterranean palates, Western teeth. But this trifold division *overruns* the three continental containers on the T-O map

(Figs. 1-2). Europe and Asia get throats and teeth, but where's the Mediterranean? And Africa?

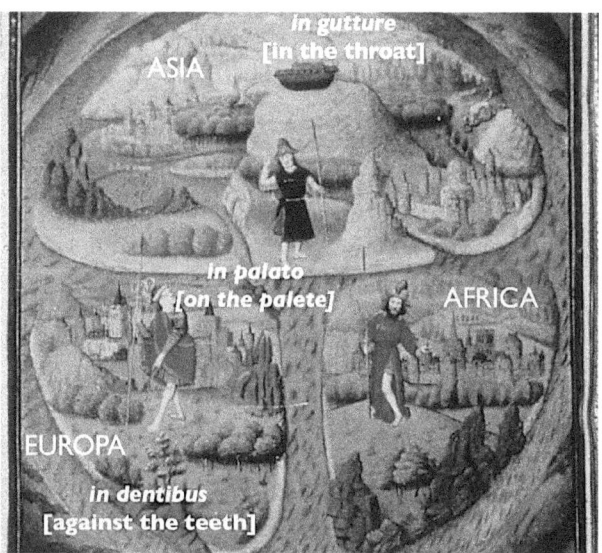

But there I go again. So often, I think about form, and rules, and broken rules. So often, I break the rules, by thinking about form instead of content. So often, I talk about form, and let others talk about content. And I imagine that talking about form and talking about content are, somehow, in some sense, equivalent. I was trained as a poet, a particular sort of poet—as a maker and breaker of the rules of language—and I am still translating myself from a poet-container to a scholar-container. I am translating myself from one reliquary to another.

And here I go back to language-containers. Dante's languages are a dysfunctional family. Three romance languages spoken by the *Franci* ("French"), *Ypsani* ("Spanish"), and *Latini* ("Italians") share common descent from Latin (*De vulgari eloquentia*, I.viii.6). Lands of *oil*, *oc*, and *si* would seem to map onto France, Spain, and Italy, but these language families *overrun* modern borders: *oil* occupies *northern* France; *oc* traverses the borders of northern Spain and southern France, and *si* is uttered across Iberia *and* Italy. [The domain of *io*, meanwhile, extends from the mouth of the Danube to Britain, encompassing modern-day England, Germany, Hungary, and Slavic areas (I.viii.4)] (Fig. 3).

Figure 3. Dante Aligheri, *De vulgaria eloquentia*: trifold model mapping onto modern nation-states (above), and the messier medieval reality Dante outlines (below). Full Latin text available online at The Latin Library: http://www.thelatinlibrary.com/dante.html.

We make rules to make containers. The rule that each section consists of one hundred words, that each section is separated by a boundary marker, that each section switches between roman and italic type—these rules create the container that holds this moment of communication. This moment creates an ad hoc, *temporally estranged community. When this was performed, the audience all heard the same words at more or less the same time, but soon after scattered. Now, you tenuous community of readers, you are all scattered from the outset. And your thin community of readers reading this section ends . . . here.*

Medieval writers theorize language-communities in an *ad hoc* fashion. Froissart, Flemish-born chronicler writing in French about travels in England, encounters an English knight who thinks him a Frenchman since he speaks *langue d'oil* (Fig. 4). Froissart records a case of mistaken "contree ou nation"—an acknowledgment that neither *lingua* nor *contree* can be fully contained by any geographically grounded *nation*.

Froissart's *Chronicles:* Inter(mis)perceptions

> Le chevalier [anglais]...Messire Guillaume de l'Ile, me vit estranger et des marches de France -- car toutes gens de la langue d'oil, de quelque contrée ou nation qu'ils soient, ils les tiennent Franchois...

Froissart's *Chronicles:* Inter(mis)perceptions

> The English knight Sir William de Lisle saw that I was [saw me as] a foreigner from the marches of France -- for all who speak the *langue d'oil* are by the English considered as French, whatever country or nation [*contrée ou nation*] they may come from ...

Figure 4. French text adapted from Jean Froissart, *Les Chronicles*, Vol. III, ed. J.A.C. Buchon (Paris, 1835), Book IV, 199. English translation from Geoffrey Brereton (ed. and trans.), *Froissart: Chronicles* (Penguin, 1978), 405.

> "*A celuy que pluys eyme en mounde,*
> *Of alle tho that I have founde*
>   *Carissima,*
> *Saluz od treyé amour,*
> *With grace and joye and alle honoure,*
>   *Dulcissima.*"

We make rules to make containers, but we also make containers to make rules. You can't rhyme across English, French, and Latin, as in this anonymous fifteenth-century poem, without first having containers for English, French, and Latin. You can't switch between the voices of two people, such as in the twenty-first century para-academic essay that you are reading, without first having a container for each voice, such as a Chris-container and a Jonathan-container.

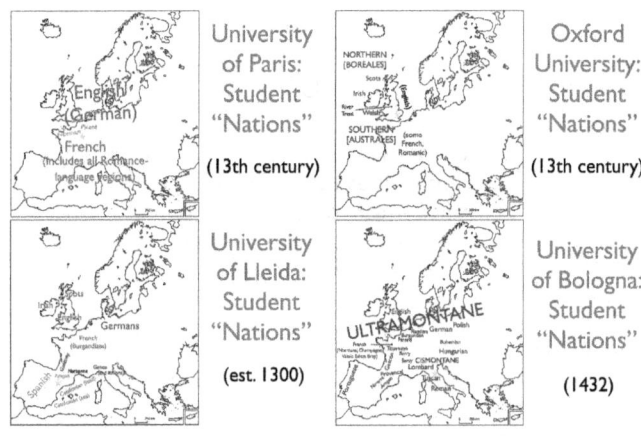

Figure 5. Geographical range of student "nations" across various medieval universities. Information collated from Pearl Kibre, *The Nations in Medieval Universities* (Cambridge: Medieval Academy of America, 1948), 179–180.

How did medieval institutions contain a polyglot world? University "nations" did *not* fix origins by geography but formed ad hoc *linguistic* containers, gathering students by their own "zero point of orientation."[1] In France, this

---

[1] Sara Ahmed, *Queer Phenomenology: Orientations, Objects, Oth-*

meant drawing fine distinctions between Picardy, Normans, other northern groups; in England, groupings took shape along a North/South divide; in Iberia, a modified Dantean scheme was in operation; and in Italy, an Alpine barrier segregated collectivities of peoples (Fig. 5). Such containers *create nations* and shape lived reality (housing, social life, governance).

Most medievalists will be quite familiar with the fourfold interpretation of scripture, whereby scripture could be read in its literal, allegorical, moral, or anagogical senses (see Fig. 6 for an allegorical reading of it). I want to propose a not quite similar fourfold interpretation of containers, which I will discuss over the next four sections. The fourfold interpretations are as follows: First, containers can be assembled ad hoc, but, second, they can also be naturalized and historicized; third, containers can keep things separate in order to allow comparison, but, fourth, they can also destabilize any attempt at comparison by overflowing.

The fourfold interpretation of scripture

Figure 6. The fourfold interpretation of scripture.

---

ers (Durham: Duke University Press, 2006), 8.

Thank you for being a friend. When medieval *Europe imagined itself as a whole* it confected *provisional* nations, quirky gatherings of friends and neighbors. See in Fig. 7 the papal bull of Benedict XII (1366), and also the consolidated voting blocs of the Council of Constance (1418).

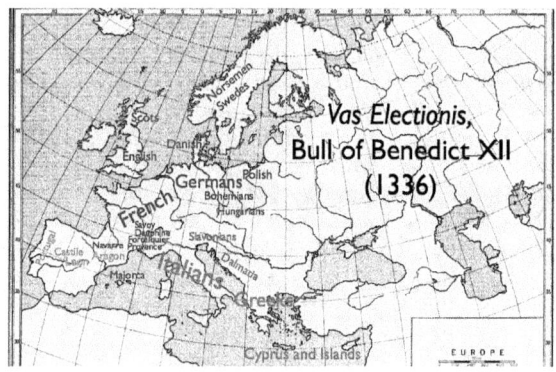

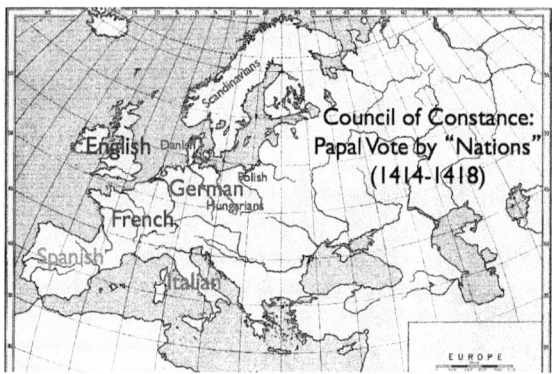

Figure 7. Above, fourfold division of "nations" (French, German, Spanish, Italian) in the *Vas Electionis* of Benedict XII (1336); below, a new "English" nation-container emerges in the Council of Constance (1414-1418).

First: Ad hoc. *Let us propose that a container can be assembled by proposing the rules of its containment. Simply by recognizing or proposing distinctions, differentiations, or family resemblances, we can separate this from that. We can make English English and French French. Let us similarly define the Chris-container as the person who wrote this italicized text about containers, and the Jonathan-container as the person who wrote the following non-italicized text that will disagree with this section. Let us, for the moment (without worrying about whether it will be possible to unthink this), think of these two persons as separate.*

Or let's not. We're all *groups* too. What does our voice mean for *collective* containers? The Modern Language Association of America (MLA), the largest professional organization in the United States for scholars of language and literature, continues to enact its own form of *divisio linguarum*. It establishes nation- and language-based membership divisions (including historical periods within "American Literature," "English Literature," "French Literature," and the like), and these categories in turn guide institutional practice.[2] Where does the scholar of Flemish literature find a home? Or Occitan? Or multilingual poetry?

Or, second: The now suddenly always already. We can insist that a container has some sort of naturalized justification. There are several tools we can use to achieve this: "nature," "common sense," "the obvious"—but we can also use "history." English is English because we can connect it, thanks to history, to the language spoken in England 1400 years ago—an England that is itself recognized as a container, defined as where English was spoken 1400 years ago. Chris is Chris because he has never stopped being the Chris that was created 38 years ago, and good luck arguing otherwise.

Yes, Chris is Chris, a living past into the present. But we're not *supposed* to be talking history but the future. So the future I want ... is *more medieval.* If medieval language-categories were overlapping and messy, why can't we *embrace* this mess?

---

[2] For a complete list of the current MLA divisions, see http://mla.org/divisions.

Which leads me to third: Connections. The container is a system that fosters comparisons and connections with other containers, and these connections proliferate beyond those initials distinctions that created these containers. Once we have the habit of thinking of English and French as contained, we can draw an infinite amount of lines to connect, contrast, or coordinate them. English tastes bitter, whereas French tastes sweet. English sounds grey, whereas French sounds cerulean. Chris and Jonathan can write an essay, or an infinite amount of essays, on any number of topics, with any number of dynamics, together—because they are apart.

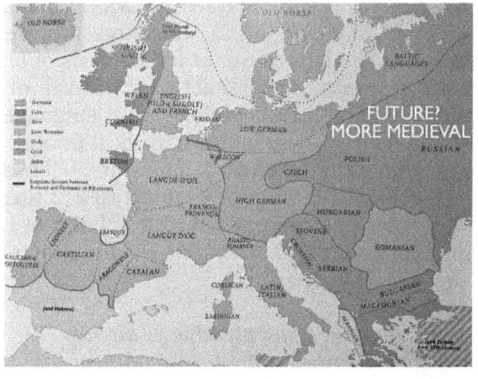

Figure 8. Linguistic landscapes, medieval and neo-medieval. Map above adapted from Rosemond McKitterick, *Atlas of the Medieval World* (Oxford University Press, 2004), 115. Bottom: See "The Languages of the Great Europe" [*sic*] and other maps at the Eurominority website: http://www.eurominority.eu/version/maps/map-european-languages.asp.

Comparisons, connections, together: Eurominority (www.eurominority.org) advocates for minority language rights beyond co/official languages and bounded nation-states. This is truly *neomedieval* thinking: any shared *lingua* is affective *natio* (Fig. 8).

Finally, fourth: Overflow. Containers overflow. They slosh. They pour forth. Even if they have to overflow with emptiness, they will overflow. Containers erode or break down or get repurposed as new types of shelter. Things fall apart; the container cannot hold. You can read Chaucer and be confused, at times, whether you're reading English or French. What are you reading? You are reading slosh. This is the rule that breaks the rule, or rather, the rule whose implications break the rule. This is the hope that when Chris and Jonathan alternate their voices, a third spectral voice might also speak.

Let's make spectral polyvocality thrive *within* containers. If MLA divisions contain us, let's fill these temporal confines with *NOISE:* in Old English let's do Celtic, Norse, Latin; in Middle English let's do all varieties, Anglo-Norman, Dutch, Latin (Fig. 9).

Figure 9. Augmented screenshot of online listing of MLA divisions (May 2013): http://www.mla.org/divisions.

This overflow—and this noise—of course it appeals to my poet-container, who creates rules to see how they can be broken, who creates rules that ensure that they will be broken. But I want to suggest that all containers, however they were constructed, can be read and reread in any of these four ways. I want the future of containers—the future of scholars dealing with containers, the future of scholars dealing with themselves as contained within their scholar-containers—to be one that is limber at moving between them, but quick to ensure that these four containers also overflow.

I want a future where containers overflow, where medieval English divisions aren't consolidated, and divisions *expand* to endless new configurations. Let's *overpopulate* our containers! Let's make MLA *more* than the MLA of Anglophone North America.

MOOD CHANGE/
COLLECTIVE CHANGE

Julian Yates and Julie Orlemanski

MOOD CHANGE (JULIAN)

for Vincent Gillespie, whose lessons still inspire

991. Here Ipswich was raided; and very soon after that Ealdorman Byrhtnoth was killed at Maldon, and in that year it was first decided tax be paid to the Danish men because of the great terror which they wrought along the sea coast. That was at first 10 thousand pounds. Archbishop Sigeric decided on the decision.[1]

---

[1] *The Anglo-Saxon Chronicle*, trans. and ed. Michael Swanton (London: J. M. Dent, 1996), 127. The quotation comes from The Canterbury Manuscript F. An alternative version of the year appears in Manuscript (E): "Here Ealdorman Bryhtnoth was killed at Maldon, and in the same year it was first decided that tax be paid to the Danish men because of the enormities which they wrought

The year 991 will never be complete. It endures, subject to remaking and revision.[2] At the time, the year must have been anticipated, welcomed, dreaded. Seasons change. Years turn. And by their passage those who live on stand recruited as mnemotechnical relays to their passing. The future, the effect of the future is never wanting, never lacking. The future happens all the time. You and we, as well as the life cycles or runtime of all its variously animated wetware (animals, plants, fungus, machines), all that "lives on," constitute the medium by which, in which, the future presences.[3] The dead stand recruited also, "dying on" by way of memory, external memory devices (memorials, tombs, etc.) and resuscitated into the fictive or factish uses of things deemed "past" in successive presents. Liveliness finds itself distributed across the continuum, from which notions of life and death, past, present, and future, find themselves extracted. The humanities cohabit with the charnel house of the collective. Our readings perform variously secular or sacred resurrections.[4]

Here, in the *Anglo-Saxon Chronicle*, the year 991 finds itself transcribed or translated according to a regime of description that we can only partially access and that manifests differently in its multiple manuscripts (A through H). The *Chronicle* inventories the eventfulness of the year; names names (Ipswich, Maldon, Byrhtnoth, Sigeric); remarks the narrative-building precedents (the first paying of a tax or tribute) along with its author, the agent that gives the advice, who decides the decision ("*ræd*

---

along the sea coast. That was the first ten thousand pounds. Archbishop Sigeric decided on the decision." For this variation, *The Anglo-Saxon Chronicle*, 126.

[2] On the concept of a year as continually subject to remaking, the year never being "finished," see Bruno Latour's discussion of "backward causation" in Bruno Latour, *Pandora's Hope: Essays on the Reality of Science Studies* (Cambridge: Harvard University Press, 1999), 168–173.

[3] On "wetware" as the biosemiotic factor to media platforms and technologies, see Richard Doyle, *Wetwares: Experiments in Post-Vital Living* (Minneapolis: University of Minnesota Press, 2003).

[4] On the "factish" as the putative entity that fractures into what we more readily process as "fact" and "fetish," an entity irreducibly "made" (fiction) but also with referential power, see Bruno Latour, *On the Modern Cult of the Factish Gods*, trans. Catherine Porter and Heather Maclean (Cambridge: Harvard University Press, 2010), 1–66.

gerædde")—the repetition or redundancy of the word "advise" or "decide" emphasizing the magnitude of the act, the "cut" or cutting that finishes one moment and inaugurates a new and escalating present as the tax exceeds its serial repetition and grows. The *Chronicle* captures also the affective geography of the country, the "enormities," "wonders" or "spectacles" ("*wundræn*" in MS F) or the "great terror" ("*mycclan brogan*" in MS E) "by the seacoast."[5] The tax figures an outward flow of resources indexed to the affective inundation of the coast. But it does not see off the terror exactly so much as it introduces an attenuated temporality. The present seems frozen, static, hollowed out by the anticipation of violence. Oriented to a future no one wants, the present is found wanting, goes missing, freezes, hostage to a serial repetition. Time pools.

Enter whomever it was that wrote or commissioned or codified or merely copied the burned fragment of a poem we call "The Battle of Maldon." In the poem, Bryhtnoth dies on, lives on, sur-vives into the present future, beyond the *Chronicle*'s announcement of his demise. And whatever the circumstances of the battle, which this poem revises and replays, this time round he's mad and moody, out to effect a mood change that might also render a mode of collective change. Bryhtnoth orders his men to dismount; marshals them. Metaphorical falcons fly from hands. Things are getting serious. No time for sport. The seafarers ask for their tax. "And it is better for you all that you should buy off this onslaught of spears with tribute money," says their spokesman in one translation, "we are prepared to establish a truce in return for gold."[6] Do yourselves a favor. Disperse; dispense your gold; and save yourselves the shock and awe, the "onslaught" we shall bring. But Bryhtnoth's having none of it; speaks for his men; for his people; offers a tax or tribute of "spears . . . deadly points and tried swords / payment in war-gear which shall be of no benefit to you in battle to pay you, pierce, slit, and slay you in storming battle" (46–47).

The battle begins, or it would, if the sea and the river

---

[5] See *The Anglo-Saxon Chronicle: A Collaborative Edition*, Vol. 8, MS F, ed. Peter S. Baker (Cambridge: D. S. Brewer, 2000), 86, and Vol. 7, MS E, ed. Susan Irvine, 61.

[6] *The Battle of Maldon*, ed. Donald Scragg (Manchester, UK: Manchester University Press, 1991), 19, lines 31–33. Subsequent references appear parenthetically in the text, cited by line number.

Panta didn't get in the way; arrest the fray; "Because of the water there, neither group could reach the other: / there the flood tide had come after the ebb, / the tidal streams had locked up the land. It seemed too long to them / to the time when they could wield spears against one another" (64–67). And so they wait; their desire for battle pooling, stayed and augmented by the delay; amped and amping up. This waiting, a product of the locale, of the environs, of the agency of the flood, figures also a replaying of or reply to the escalating series that is, that was, the tax. The carefully reckoned tax that decides, that cuts or cross cuts the present finds itself overwritten by this other pooling of desire, of an anticipation that is already completed, finished and that awaits expression merely. Violence shall erupt and rewrite the present by an expenditure of flesh become poetic affect. The terror wrought by the sea coast, a sea coast affectively re-written by the seafarers finds itself answered in kind, reversed or, better still, rejoined by its like, pushing outwards.[7]

Such a mood change as it courses through Bryhtnoth and his men proves uncritical, post-critical. It cannot know as it does, even as it might seek to know as it becomes. Its emphatic singularity leaves it open to doubt, to criticism, reappraisal, reprisal. Bryhtnoth will be judged to have yielded too much ground: his too-much-ness will condense into pride. The seafarers (guileful or gleeful) see the problem—advancing along a narrow and defended causeway leaves them at a serious tactical disadvantage;

---

[7] For a revisionist reading of the poem that calls its criticism of the tax and accordingly its date into question, see Leonard Neidorf, "Aethlred and the Politics of the Battle of Maldon," *JEGP* 111.4 (October 2012): 451–473. Neidorf takes the poem's relative equanimity towards the seafarers or Vikings in its representations to be at odds with a project of direct political intervention or criticism and asks readers to rethink the poem's relation to the politics of the 990s. Neidorf's argument is persuasive, but I would suggest that the poem's recuperation of the moment of battle and the active seeking after death following the death of one's lord or leader reprograms the act of participating in battle as an aesthetic, mythic end in and of itself. Accordingly, the seafarers are necessary agents in making good on this death-seeking and death-loving endeavor. On the mythic function of the poem see, John D. Niles, "Maldon and Mytho-poesis," in *Old English Literature: Critical Essays*, ed. R.M. Liuzza (New Haven: Yale University Press, 2002), 445–474.

and so they ask to cross in order to join battle. "Because of his pride" (89) or "overconfidence" ("*ofermode*"), Bryhtnoth allows them to do so. The word defies parsing or parses too much, signifying an "over" or "too much" heart or mood. And this "too-much-ness" proves key. For I am not interested in whether Bryhtnoth did right or wrong. Instead, I venture that the script the poem follows aims to reverse the tax, and by advocating for an aesthetic response *in extremis*, orchestrates a super- or over-plus, a plus-sized writing or over-writing of his present. Mood change. "*Mod*" change. Collective change.

Bryhtnoth dies; Godwine and Godwig flee, "turned from the fight and sought the wood, / they fled into that place of safety and saved their lives" (193–194); but the hostage stays, Bryhtnoth's men rally; live on; die on (with him); moral philsophemes, patterns of a variously anachronistic heroic ideal, summoned to do service in a present that aims to produce altered futures. Bryhtnoth's "*ofermode*" or "too-much-ness" spills beyond his veins, an ecstatic drug that courses through the collective. His example in battle provides a template for the actions that follow, for the further recruitment of his men who live on or die on with him. The poem serves a delivery tool for this rhetorical pattern or software, equipment for living and dying, input for an aesthetic, affective re-education but not quite a counter-pedagogy.[8] The mode it employs offers a joyful, violent, courting of limits, writing beyond or into the limits, which it aims to over-flow and so to rewrite the rules for making futures. Bryhtnoth, while he lives, is all noise. He bellows. He laughs, party to a jocund, sadomasochistic splendor or spectacle as he faces off with the "warrior" who's first to wound him—to their mutual delight (134–139). Such is the hypnotizing high of tuning yourself to the hyper-reference of a world configured to the limit, as Bryhtnoth offers, that limit, that risk, the aesthetic heft required to the undoing of a decision, the further cutting of the cut to the present, the tax that weighs upon the future.[9]

---

[8] For this modeling of literary texts as equipment, see Kenneth Burke "Literature and Equipment for Living," in *The Philosophy of Literary Form*, 3rd edn. (Berkeley: University of California Press, 1973), 293–304.

[9] On the homoerotic/homophobic quotient to the exchange with the warrior—sometimes translated as "churl," "peasant," or

Byrhtwold, who speaks and dies last, just before the poem cuts out, names the orientation Bryhtnoth embodies and requires. He condenses the script; returns us to the word *mod*, which he inclines towards the more, to moreness, offering a recipe for the constitution of an *ofermode*:

Hyge sceal þy heardra,   heorte þy cenre,
mod sceal þy mare   þy ure mæg˙en lytlap.

[The spirit must be the firmer, the heart the bolder, courage must be the greater, as our strength diminishes.] (312–313)

Marking and inhabiting the death of his lord, which serves as the limit to his own living on, Bryhtwold prescribes the rate or quotient to the affect of the moment. Mood must augment, must incline towards the more. "Courage must be the greater." It must augment, its rise calibrated by the rate at which "our strength diminishes." These lines prescribe what sounds like an extreme titration that linearizes a collective. The affective hits of "*ofermode*" course through them all, in series, by Bryhtnoth's cutting off and down, constituting them as a single fleshly *thing*.

The logic Bryhtwold names might then be understood already to recognize the biopolitical articulation and management of the collective as an aleatory body, as "flesh" to be variously differentiated and parceled out in different forms, to be dosed with so many rhetorical, somatic, and psychological uppers and downers.[10] As each

---

"yeoman" in lines 130–133 of the poem, see, Allen J. Frantzen, *Before the Closet: Same-Sex Love from "Beowulf" to "Angels in America"* (Chicago: University of Chicago Press, 2000), 105–106. Frantzen remains one of the most astute readers of this moment, carefully entertaining possibilities as to how the moment's choreography, the way a relationship of sorts is established between the two men, is inflected by differentials of nation, social rank, and skill. On the joy/danger/erotics of such limit testing see I draw on Leo Bersani, *The Freudian Body: Psychoanalysis and Art* (New York: Columbia University Press, 1986) and Leo Bersani and Adam Phillips, *Intimacies* (Chicago: University of Chicago Press, 2008).

[10] For this notion of governmentality and "flesh" see Roberto Esposito's recasting of Foucauldian bio-power in Roberto Esposito, *Immunitas: The Protection and Negation of Life* (London: The Polity Press, 2011), 140–141. See also, Cary Wolfe's key proposi-

of Bryhtnoth's surviving men speak, we hear the process by which he finds himself constituted as part of a single fleshly *thing*, subject to a biopolitical articulation of the collective as "flesh" to be variously drugged up and parceled out in different forms (which includes its listeners and readers, then and now). Here, that flesh finds itself well and truly dosed. And so Anglo-Saxon flesh is configured to answer the undifferentiated inundation of Seafarers.

What then do we learn from this poem with regard to the future/s we want? Coming after the battle even as it replays it, "The Battle of Maldon" rewrites the event at Maldon as already, before the fact, a refusal of the tax and it does so in mythic and mythologizing mode, marshaling a set of aesthetic forces to its end and so offers a lesson in the rhetorical efficacy to be claimed by the looping, pooling, and re-orientation of relations between our successive "nows." The poem rewires the meaning of that day in 991 when battle was joined at Maldon, and in so doing seeks to intervene in the way the year is archived. But the poem's violent, lyrical, ecstatic, coercive mode and mood remains almost entirely neutral. The poem offers no viable mimetic politics. Instead, it documents the process by which Bryhtnoth's constitutive "too-much-ness" orchestrates a violent, mimetic over-writing of individual bodies as it collectivizes the group, literally marshals them to its martial ends. The poem offers, at best, an ambivalent set of pleasures, a time-bound belonging, as it translates the violence of the battle as event into its own semiotic and lyric "flesh," which it offers to its readers.

Fragment from a burned manuscript, the poem offers no exits; no products; even as it produces a set of material and affective changes among the men it depicts. The lesson lies not in the positing of an image a particular kind of future, filling in the future before the fact—such was the time machine that Sigeric authored with the tax for which he advocated. Instead, the poem offers a hyper-awareness and orientation to the present, to the now-time of decision, pitting itself against a moment that has passed by and to which it emphatically insists that we return. Then again, there is the figure of the pause that comes with the river Panta and the sea:

---

tions in *Before the Law* (Chicago: University of Chicago Press, 2013).

> Because of the water there, neither group could reach the other:
> there the flood tide had come after the ebb,
> the tidal streams had locked up the land. It seemed too long to them
> to the time when they could wield spears against one another. (64–67)

For battle to be joined, for the future the poem finds lacking to find itself un- or over-written, the human participants to the action, the "flesh" or wetware of the poem, have to agree to a crossing. They momentarily join forces against the land and the water that come between and that stall or arrest the action. What then if we allowed these watery agents, the river and the sea, to rebel against their brute physicality or apparent metaphoricity in the poem, and so to manifest as some third thing, a third force that interrupts and stays the action of the poem and its world? When the tide ebbs, both sides must agree to fight, must work together in order to make battle possible. Anglo-Saxon and seafarer flesh accommodate the other. How then to identify and occupy those moments when this third thing, the environs, what comes between, ebb away, and appears to offer us unfettered decisions? How to understand these localized, time-bound moments, keyed to the infrastructures we inhabit as renewable nodes of radical choice, a choice whose possibility and openness the poem archives even as it decides?[11]

Once upon a time, it was all the rage for readers and critics of "The Battle of Maldon" as well as serious archaeologists of to visit Northey, in Essex, and to cross or edge up to the causeway and even to re-enact the poem in order to discover if Bryhtnoth and the spokesman for the seafarers really could have called back and forth to each other over the water. Even as such antiquarian longing may raise hackles or induce wry smiles, the pedestrian

---

[11] It is precisely this moment of human misrecognition, the reduction of the world to an obstacle to human violence, with which Michel Serres begins *The Natural Contract* as he seeks to imagine human collectives that are not predicated on the routinized forgetting of the world and the normalization of violence as part of human societies, see Michel Serres, *The Natural Contract*, trans. William Paulson and Elizabeth MacArthur (Ann Arbor: University of Michigan Press, 1992), 1–27.

traffic or fetish labor of such readers-become-travelers and re-enactors is not so very different from what today constitutes the labor of reading in what we name the humanities. Even as the register in which they understood their labor to count might have been misdirected, such antiquarian impulses to go *there* augur a certain kind of epistemological advantage to be had from the poem's sense of place, the *thisness* of the *thing* that happened *there*.[12] And it is this *thisness* or *thereness*, pseudo-deictic as it maybe, that ultimately matters.

The challenge for me and for those of us housed in the humanities, as I see it, remains tied in fostering modes of aesthetic experience, modes of perception, that enable us to access this order of proximity to *things* (places, persons, historical moments). For then, perhaps, we shall come to know and embody or feel what the river and the sea seem, in this poem, to know already, namely that power is weak. The water, keyed as it is to the affective heft of anticipation as it courses through the poem's flesh, designates the presence of a generalized flesh of being, the aleatory body that power seeks somehow to harness and manage, but which so exceeds its governmental dosing as to constitute a pure contingency, capable of generating still other futures, futures for which we have neither script nor name. I end, then, by advocating not a radical present or closure of the future as ideological lure—not "no future"—but, in a stricter framework still, an insistence on a judicious emptiness, the future something that cannot, perhaps should not, be imagined, for it resides in and is produced by the way we re/draw the relationships between texts, readings, lives, deaths, events, today.

The future is never lacking then. It wants for nothing, even as it taxes our present circumstances with its open-

---

[12] See for example such essays or book chapters reporting on the location of the battle as, George R. Petty Jr. and Susan Petty, "Geology and the Battle of Maldon," *Speculum* 51.3 (July 1976): 435–446; George and Susan Petty, "A Geological Reconstruction of the Site of the Battle of Maldon," in *The Battle of Maldon: Fact and Fiction*, ed. Janet Cooper (London: Hambledon, 1993), 161–169; O.D. Macrae-Gibson, "How Historical is the Battle of Maldon?" *Medium Ævum* 39 (1970): 89–107; John McN. Dodgson, "The Site of the Battle of Maldon," in *The Battle of Maldon*, ed. Scragg, 170–179; Roger Schmidt, "A Trip to Maldon," *Rendez-Vous* 38.2 (Spring 2004): 59–63.

ness, its radical blankness, remaining emphatically yet to be written.[13]

COLLECTIVE CHANGE (JULIE)

When Julian mentioned that he was thinking of thinking through *mood change* and *collective change* by way of the "Battle of Maldon," I thought I would try too.

But I was surprised to discover how strong my resistance ran to the changes of mood that rippled through the poem's martial collective, that flooded across those individuals as they transformed
themselves into an agglomerated *unit*
glowing brighter as bodies came undone (combusting that fragile, integral, organismal thing,
with a jubilant *there! you have it!* dying
in great sweet spiels of ideological trash,
      dense curlicues of rhetorical *manifestation*
          blowing out the dials of an austere
              and taciturn poetry. . .).

In any case, as someone who's used up dreamless nights
    dull-puzzling to think *collective change*,
I found the whole thing distasteful: the synecdochal consolidation around Byrhtnoth,
    over-hearty, mooded unto excess, *proud*,
pumped up with the supercharged selfhood
of the collective subject, making
his awesome gestures of decision
that go on being realized for a long time after,
that go on being realized even now.

Some lines from before the battle:

    Ða þær Byrhtnoð   *ongan beornas trymian,*
    rad and rædde,   *rincum tæhte*

---

[13] For a critique of "reproductive futurism" and the articulation "no future," see Lee Edelman, *No Future: Queer Theory and the Death Drive* (Durham: Duke University Press, 2004). On the need to maintain the future as strategically blank, see Karl Marx, "The Eighteenth Brumaire of Louis Bonaparte," in *The Marx and Engels Reader*, 2nd edn., ed. Robert C. Tucker (New York: W.W. Norton & Co., 1978), 595.

hu hi sceoldon standan and þone stede healdan,
and bæd þæt hyra randas rihte heoldon
fæste mid folman, and ne forhtedon na. (17-21)

[Then Byrhtnoth began to encourage them there, he rode about and gave them advice, taught the warriors how they should stand and maintain the position, and urged them to hold their shields properly, securely with their hands, and not to be afraid at all.][14]

When I read these lines (lit up as they are with the light of soft organs beneath warriors' skin), I want to tell Byrhtnoth to just *lay off*, stop the aesthetic education he never stops delivering at those junctures where we can't help but listen, lean into him, mimic his postures, let him adjust our grip and loosen our fear.

After all, it matters
what we're standing for, doesn't it?
And how the decisions are made?

There is something about how the poem's speeches go, spooling out from one body after another as each gives up its mad red soul, that makes me suspicious. Loyalty's compulsive tic, sacrifice and resacrifice:

hi woldon þa ealle oðer twega,
lif forlætan oððe leofne gewrecan. (207-208)

[they all wanted one of two things,
to give up their life or to avenge their beloved lord.]

Collective mourning works itself out
until no one's left standing but the collective itself
(the lines of light that yoked men together,
still visible *sans* men) and a great sweet cloud of mood
and the Vikings who've gone back to their ship.

In fall of 2011
I made some experiments of myself

---

[14] "The Battle of Maldon," in *Old and Middle English c.890-c.1450: An Anthology*, ed. Elaine Treharne (London: Blackwell, 2010), 156–169.

in a standing-off crowd.

At OCCUPY BOSTON I marched in marches
and shouted in public spaces where I felt the force
of not having shouted there before
and the impossibility, really, of ever shouting there alone.
I sat through very long meetings,
    distended vacuoles of *process*,
that sometimes succeeded in
engineering a sequence of voices
that made communication's unknown amplitudes ring,
the muteness of which
    I hadn't been able to specify before.
But lots of times the long meetings failed,
and I was embarrassed.

Some principles of the Occupy movement were: horizontal democracy, peaceful disobedience, radical inclusiveness, mutual aid. "Decide to be a part of this!" the thing said to me. "Decide to join up" had to keep being decided again, which made it different from the military contract of coercion and brotherhood, belonging and conscription, which has a long history of getting shit done, the Vikings remind us.

Hi bugon þa fram beaduwe þe þær beon noldon. (185)

[Then those who did not want to be there turned away from battle.]

they þone wudu sohto (193)

[they sought the woods]

Just so our protest community was excruciatingly porous,
    voluntarist;
we kept seeping out of it.
How does one decide what collective
    to change oneself into?
Not just to pledge allegiance to the land of my circumstance (to defend to death wherever already I am),
but also not to subject, say, every chant, every protest sign,
every comrade to the scrupulosity of my sniff-test, to my
hygienic, self-important decisionism . . . .

You
test the wind,
I guess,
and estimate if you still coincide
    with the collective project underway,
whatever mix of means and ends is materialized
    in the community there,
lodged like a cyst in time and space,
practicing its new pantomimes of justice.

One gets
very exhausted
when one realizes the collective won't survive the scene of its standing. And, as predicted, there is soon occasion for the trampled grass to be viciously replanted. A mural commemorates the feeling of feelings that won't be allowed to linger there.

And so one talks about it a short time after, but already far from the project whose velocity gave one's articulations sense. Which is what makes it different from heroic poetry, I suppose—from which the collective goes on glowing and emitting its moods that settle on the reader in a fine radioactive dust blown back from the year 991, still capable of being resisted and capable of being felt.

www.ingramcontent.com/pod-product-compliance
Lightning Source LLC
Chambersburg PA
CBHW071437150426
43191CB00008B/1152